Nations without God

THE DAWN OF WORLDWIDE GOVERNMENT

by Barney Fuller

Huntington House Publishers

Huntington House Publishers
P.O. Box 53788
Lafayette, Louisiana 70505

Library of Congress Card Catalog Number 95-77032
ISBN 1-56384-098-7

Printed in the U.S.A.

Contents

Foreword

Nations Without God is a book on eschatological prophecy that will make every reader "sit up and take notice." There is no doubt that the signs of the times are all around us, and we are seeing them at every hand. Yet, many Christians are not spiritually and mentally prepared for all these things which will shortly come to pass.

It is evident that a tremendous amount of research and study of the Scriptures has gone into the writing of this book. The author points out the tremendous role which the United States of America will play in the end-times.

An angel of the Lord appeared to a Christian man in South Africa recently and told him, "Jesus is coming very soon!" Let us take warning, live holy lives, and be willing to lay down our very lives for the faith; for the day of persecution has already dawned in some nations as the Devil, knowing his time is short, is going about as a roaring lion.

But the Lion of Judah has risen from the dead and He will never fail to win the contest against the powers of evil for to Him is the Kingdom, and the Power, and the Glory forever and ever. Amen.

—Gwen R. Shaw,
President of the End-Time Handmaidens

Acknowledgment

The one I wish to thank the most for assisting me in all the many details in the writing of this book is my wife Joanne. Thanks so very much for all those hours of your time.

Introduction

I believe that we have arrived at the time in history which many of the prophets have declared to be the Day of the Lord; others refer to it as the Time of the End. The prophet Daniel would, no doubt, have called it the Seventieth Week. In our day Christians look upon it as the Time of Tribulation. But, the Bible helps us to see that it is a special day, when God takes the reigns of the earth back under His full control and brings into full manifestation the mystery of His divine will.

One of the purposes of this book is to establish the validity of the Seventieth Week and to allow the reader to see the unique way in which the Lord has chosen to spotlight the beginning and ending of those seven years.

During these seven years, Satan's power over the earth will reach its zenith. What has been called the "mark of the beast" will become law worldwide. The second beast is already flexing his muscles on the earth and by the year 2000, plus or minus a few months, the organizational structure and the military commitments should be in place.

The voice of warning needs to go throughout the earth, that the nations may know of the desolating designs of Satan. But, equally important, the believer must be fully informed and spiritually prepared to face and to overcome the temptation and trial of this hour.

It is expedient that the saints thrust in the sickles of their testimony and reap while the harvest is ripe.

The Seventieth Week is designed by the Lord for the completion of His holy purposes which began in the Garden of Eden. Those purposes include the final triumph of the Church, which will be realized in the perfecting of the Bride. The Day of the Lord will take the world up to the time of the vials of God's most potent wrath, and will reach its conclusion just prior to the Battle of Armageddon.

It has been my prayer that this book will give the Christian a clear understanding as to who the first beast is, which John prophecies of in the Book of Revelation, as well as, a vivid picture of the rising of the second beast. It has been my deep desire while preparing this book that it would provide the Bride of Christ with the understanding which will help her to more effectively prepare for this hour, so that this day of tremendous deception may not come upon her as a thief in the night (Rev. 16:15).

The Mystery of Daniel's Seventieth Week: the Finding of the Year A.D. 2000

The world is gearing up for a special celebration as the twenty-first century approaches. One billion "New Agers" will celebrate the year 2000 as the end of the Christian Age, and the beginning of the Age of Aquarius where they plan to make a quantum leap into a new age of light, unity, peace, and superhuman abilities. The New Agers openly profess that the new millennium 2000 will vault their kingdom into complete control of Mother Earth. Many New World Order prophets are proclaiming that the year 2000 will bring the world under a united sovereign government. But, at the same time many Christians believe that the year 2000 will bring back the Lord Jesus Christ to set up His kingdom upon the earth.

I can understand why the New Agers, as well as, the One Worlders have chosen the year 2000 for their great moment of celebration, since they have a plan, a well laid-out strategy with the machinery in full operation to bring it all to pass. Today, all across America, school teachers are being prepared to teach their students all about the exciting powers of the occult. The children will be introduced to astral travel, which is only possible through demonic communication. They will be taught how to enter into a trance and explore occult visualization. Experimentation into clairvoyance and other extramental experiences will be on the agenda of the very young. I would expect these "well-dressed" occult programs to be in full swing before the year 2000.

There is little question that Satan has earmarked this coming new millennium as the time when he intends to take a firm grip on the world. The earth will fill with false prophets as his kingdom rises to full power in the year 2000. Jesus warned of these cultic New Age prophets and their great deceiving powers that they would so persuasively manifest.

"For there shall arise false christs, and false prophets, and shall show great signs and wonders; insomuch that, if it were possible, they shall deceive the very elect" (Matt. 24:24).

Bill Clinton, Al Gore, and the rest of the deceived world plan to amalgamate the nations of the earth into one glorious superstate at the dawning of the year 2000. The collectivizing of the earth has long been the plan of the Illuminati,* the high-ranking Masons, the Council on Foreign Relations, the Builderbergers, the Rockefellers, the Rothchilds, the United Nations, the World Council of Churches, the New Agers, the Communists, and the Socialists of America. These groups are all part of the same apple. They are intertwined; just different colored threads of the same garment. Albert Pike, former head of the Masonic Order of the Scottish Rite and the Illuminati, as well as, author of one of the most respected and honored works in Freemasonry, "Morals and Dogma," taught that Lucifer is the god of light and Jesus Christ is the God of darkness, and that the day would finally come when the

---

*The Illuminati is a secret Luciferic order founded in Ingolstadt, Bavaria (Germany) on 1 May 1776 by Adam Weishaupt, a Freemason. The infiltration of high-ranking Masons into the governments of the whole world is staggering.

pure doctrine of Lucifer would be brought out into public view. This manifestation according to Pike will bring about the destruction of Christianity.

In contrast the Christians have no such plan or machinery in the works, they have a hope that the year 2000 may be the year that the Lord will return. But, if that be not the year of the Lord's return, they have the sure promise that He will not leave them nor forsake them.

The prophet Amos tells us, "Surely the Lord God will do nothing, but he revealeth His secret unto His servants the Prophets" (Amos 3:7). God will always impart understanding to those who seek Him with all their hearts. Albert Einstein asked a man one time what he knew for sure. Well, there is one thing for sure, and that is, the culmination of history will adjust to what the Bible has to say. The Bible is a prophetic book, wherein God has already revealed the beginning and the end. There will be no "Johnny come lately" religion, like the New Agers, which will alter the future and change the prophesied course of God's Word as foretold in the Holy Bible. They will have a party much like ancient Babylon did, but it will be divinely interrupted very shortly after it begins (Dan. 5).

The Lord desires that we walk in "His light" as the end approaches. If we do not, it will be impossible to comprehend the times and seasons of God. I believe it is vital that we come to understand when the year 2000 will occur on God's clock. What the world does not realize is that God is the only true keeper of time. He has ordered and synchronized the minutes, hours, days, months, and years just as He has ordered the planets and the stars, and has long before decreed when the end shall be. God alone is the orchestrator of time for the world. There will be no quantum leap in the year 2000 as the New Agers prophesy. What will be, is a giant leap by the world into the devil's snare of deception. Because, time emanates from God, the world's leap will not occur in His year of 2000.

When Adam was created the history of man began to move toward a time which God had appointed; a predetermined time in which He would redeem the world. That time was set by God just as deliberately as the reader would set a clock. God's clock for this earth began to tick the day He created man, and there are some students of the Bible who believe that from the birth of Adam to the birth of the nation of Israel there was reckoned a period of two thousand years; and from the birth of the nation of Israel to the birth of Jesus there would be another two thousand years.

It is interesting to note that halfway between the birth of Jesus and Jacob, David would be born. Also, it is interesting to note that David was born halfway between the beginning and the end. He was Israel's first and only prophet and king. He was a prototype of the prophesied Messiah. He was a man after God's own heart. The foregoing is evidence enough to believe that God has something very special in His plans for the year 2000. His two thousandth year will end September 1996 on His calendar.

God gave the world two thousand years after the birth of the nation of Israel to prepare for His first coming into the world, and the last set of two thousand years to learn of Him and prepare for the day of His second coming. Since we are fast approaching the end of the two thousandth year, it should deeply behoove us to want to know what time it is on the clock of God; particularly since Jesus told the Jews that they knew not the time of their visitation (Luke 19:44). The Jews missed the coming of their God.

The Bible tells us that the earth is the Lord's and the fullness thereof. Therefore, God as the creator has to be the unseen cause which is directing the course of history to its final hour. The Bible tells us that God has

appointed a time in which He will judge the world
(Acts 17:31). The prophet Daniel tells us that the end
of the world has been appointed by God (Dan. 11:35).
In other words, God has a predetermined time set
when He will cause time, as we know it, to be no
longer (Rev. 10:6).

The Scriptures have vividly warned us not to become dependent upon our wisdom, but to always look
unto God. But, to receive God's wisdom we must first
receive His spirit. The Holy Spirit is the earnest of our
redemption. In other words, it is one of the vital rea-
sons Jesus came. The Apostle Paul helps us to understand. "Now we have received, not the spirit of the
world, but the spirit which is of God; that we might
know the things that are freely given to us of God. But,
the natural man receiveth not the things of the spirit
of God: for they are foolishness unto Him: neither can
he know them, because they are spiritually discerned"
(1 Cor. 2:12, 14).

I have no doubt in my mind that God wants His
people to share His understanding, respecting the closing of this dispensation and to possess sound scriptural
knowledge which pertains to the time of the end, so
that the "end" shall not come upon the child of God
"unawares" (Luke 21:34).

The date and time of the birth of Jesus was a divine
"mandate" and the central most important day in God's
great schematic "blueprint" of history. The timing of
the birth of Jesus was very crucial in the plan of God,
because Jesus was the chosen prophetic vertex which
all else pointed to and was centered from. The angel
of heaven marked the day when he declared, "For unto
you is born this day in the city of David a saviour,
which is Christ the Lord" (Luke 2:11). It was a holy
moment: it set the date when the "light" began to
divide the darkness; when the breath of God again was
breathed into the world. The seed of woman had

sprouted, as it were, out of dry ground. All heaven watched as the Lamb of God was born. The long awaited spotless blood, which had the power to save, had arrived at last. It was on the first day of the Jewish new year, the Bible called it the fullness of time. A new millennium had begun! The eternal God had physically stepped into the history of men (1 Tim. 3:16).

The day that Jesus was born was a day of the holy gathering, known as Rosh Hashanah, the Feast of Trumpets. This day on the Jewish calender is the first day of the new year. But, most certainly, it was the day that the Lord had made. This day in Jewish tradition is one of sweetness, when apples are dipped in honey. It was the day that the rabbis taught that the Messiah would come.

In the Gospel of John 1:1, 14 we read, "In the beginning was the Word, . . . and the Word was God. . . . And the Word was made flesh." The birth of Jesus Christ in the Jewish month of Tishri in 5 B.C., fulfilled centuries of prophecy, since the days of Adam.

To establish this date of 5 B.C., let us turn to the historian Josephus. He records the death of Herod as having occurred just before the feast of Passover in a year in which there was a full eclipse of the moon. Josephus tells us that Herod's death occurred a few days after the eclipse (Josephus XVII, VI. 4, p. 365). It had been scientifically determined that the lunar eclipse happened on the night of March 13 in the year of 4 B.C. Herod died a few months after Jesus was born.

The ministry of Jesus covered a period of 1260 days or three-and-a-half years. He began His ministry on the Great Day of Feasts in the month of Tishri (September—October, A.D. 25) and continued until He was crucified at the feast of Passover (A.D. 29) on Wednesday the day before high Sabbath (John 19:31) or exactly three-and-a-half years later. If we subtract the three-and-a-half years from March of A.D. 29 (Passover) when He was crucified, it will bring us back to September—October of A.D. 25. The birth of Jesus not only would signal the ending of the four thousand years since Adam, but, would trumpet the beginning of the last two thousand years allotted to man. These two thousand years have been looked upon as the last age.

By God's clock, the age of Adam was the first two thousand years; the age of the nation Israel was the second two thousand years; and the age of the Messiah was the third two thousand years.

Shortly before the year 2000 B.C., God changed Jacob's name to Israel, and bestowed Abraham's blessing upon him at Bethel. A few weeks later Rachael gave her life in Bethlehem giving birth to Benjamin, the twelfth son of Jacob. We see that it was in Bethlehem that the last son of Israel was born. The son was named Benjamin, which means "son of the right hand," which would foretell of the coming of God's Son which sits on the right hand of the Father. He too, would be born in Bethlehem.

Jesus said, "I am Alpha and Omega, the beginning and the end, the first and the last" (Rev. 22:13). Therefore there is none other who could be the beginning of these last two millenniums. He would be the one or the "stone cut out of the mountain (God's domain) without hand" (Dan. 2:34).

Therefore, to decide the date when the last two thousand years will end, we need only to take the time when Jesus was born in September of 5 B.C. and add that date to two thousand years. This would bring us to the end of the year 2000 (on the secular calendar September 1996). This date of September 1996 is the first day of the Jewish new year, called Rosh Hashanah. The two thousandth year since the birth of Jesus will end on this special Jewish festival day in September of 1996. This month, called Tishri on the Jewish calendar, marks the end of the old year and brings in the new year of 1996.

It is the author's belief that the seventieth week of
Daniel's prophecy will begin at that time and will con-
clude seven years later on the same Jewish new year in
A.D. 2003.

The last seven years will bring complete fulfillment
to the seventieth week of the revelation given by Gabriel
to Daniel (Dan. 9:27). This last prophetic week of seven
years will separate the sixth millennium from the seventh millennium. The sixth millennium, as the author
views, will conclude in 1996 in the month of Tishri on
Rosh Hashanah. The seventh millennium, or the one
thousand year reign of Christ, will begin seven years
later.

It was on the eighth day that Jesus was circumcised.
The cutting away symbolized the cleansing of the person. When the seventh year of Daniel's seventieth week
shall end, the eighth year (since 1996) will begin. Jesus
will, on the eighth day circumcise the earth, He will cut
away all that offends and is unclean.

In Revelation 11:3, we see that a special covenant
witness of the gospel shall be preached for a period of
three-and-a-half years. Then the beast will attack the
servants of God. In Revelation 13:5, it states that this
beast will be given power to continue for three-and-a-
half years during which time he will make war against
the saints of God.

In Revelation 20:4, we read that those who do not
embrace the religious and political philosophy of the
beast, but resist him for those three-and-a-half years in
which he will reign, will live and reign with Christ one
thousand years. This verse in Revelation 20:4 reveals
that the millennium reign of Christ does not start until
after the three-and-a-half years reign of the beast ends.

These two episodes together create a period of
seven years (three-and-a-half of the last witness of the
gospel and three-and-a-half of the beast's reign). This
seventieth week starts at the close of the sixth millen-

nium (1996) and will end at the beginning of the seventh millennium (2003), thus, creating a gap of seven
years between the two millenniums. I believe this week
to be the time which is called the Day of the Lord,
Jacob's Trouble, the Time of Tribulation and the Great
and Last Day.

This Jewish new year of 1996 (Rosh Hashanah) not
only marks the end of the 6000 years which God allotted to man, but, trumpets the beginning of the seven
years in which God would bring a full end to all nations and usher in the kingdom of His Son. We can see
it more clearly on the following chart:

Daniel's Seventieth Week—7 years

1996   2003

First 3½ Years	Last 3½ Years
Last Witness of the Gospel	Reign of the Beast

During this time, we shall see that God has set
these years apart for Himself to:

1. Finish the witness of the gospel
2. Bring in everlasting righteousness
3. Separate the wheat from the tares
4. Permit the union of the first and second beast
5. Permit the mark of the beast to run its course
6. Permit the rapture of the Bride
7. Allow the abomination which will bring desolation to be set up
8. Have Armageddon follow some time after the
   rapture. (This is discussed in a later chapter.)

I believe the seventieth week of Daniel will commence with a new and special anointing of the Spirit
provided especially by God as the Scriptures testify:
"For He will finish the work, and cut it short in righteousness: because a short work will the Lord make
upon the earth" (Rom. 9:28). This same seventieth week

will conclude in glory seven years later with the rapture of the Bride of Christ very near to the beginning of their Jewish new year in 2003. I believe this seven year period will begin exactly two thousand years from the day that the Word was made flesh in Bethlehem, and began to dwell among us.

Chapter Two

The Wise Shall Understand, Daniel 12:10

Throughout the Bible we can find God utilizing many various cycles of years through which He performed His works. I believe that God chose in the writing of the final chapter of this world's history, to place great emphasis upon cycles divisible by seven. God has strongly verified this by placing the death of Jesus into a cycle of seven, as well as the beginning of the "seventy week" prophecy given to Daniel. The amazing part is, the beginning of the first week and the last week of the "seventy week" prophecy are both intersected by the same unbroken seventy year cycle which began when Cyrus, king of Persia, gave the commandment to build and restore Jerusalem in 524 B.C.

Seven has been God's numerical expression which has testified of His perfecting hand at work. His fingerprints can be seen inter-lacing His own timetable into the historical process of the world which He has made. There is little question that the number seven has found great favor in God's Word.

The usage of seven begins in Genesis and does not cease until we reach the twenty-first chapter of the Book of Revelation. In the Book of Revelation, seven has been utilized by the spirit of God fifty-four times. There are twenty groups of sevens, such as the seven churches, the seven candlesticks, the seven seals, the

seven angels, the seven trumpets, etc. Perhaps the twenty
groupings were testifying of the twenty centuries which
would come and go before Christ would come again.

It is in the seventieth week of Daniel's prophecy
that so many of the "sevens of God" are found inter-
secting at the beginning and ending of that prophetic
week. Each of the seven days in Genesis, which speaks
of the Creation, most likely represent a thousand years
for each day. We also see this drama reenacted in the
history of man, where man was given six days (six
thousand years) of time, and shortly after it transpires,
God's seventh day Sabbath or the millennial reign of
Christ will begin.

In Genesis we read that Jacob served Laban seven •
days, which as we know, was a period of seven years on
each occasion. We witness here a double emphasis on
the seven year period of time in which the Lord will
specifically be focusing and preparing to receive His
Bride. Naman had to dip seven times in the river Jordan before God would cleanse him. When God brings
His Church out of modern Babylon, she'll spend seven
years immersed in the waters of Jesus' blood before
she will put on the white linen, and become as a chaste
virgin (Rachel),* prepared as a bride for the Lamb of
God. John tells us that he saw a lamb in the midst of
the throne of God as if it had been slain, which had
seven horns. I believe one of those horns of divine
power represented the Blood of the Lamb. During
Daniel's seventieth week, our understanding of the
blood of Jesus and its purifying and resurrecting power
will be infinitely enhanced.

---

*Leah, Jacob's first wife, symbolized the first church in the
Old Testament; Rachel, the second wife, the bride of the
New Testament church.

The following prophetic chart reveals how God has so ordered the events of history and so decreed them, after the counsel of His own wisdom, that time itself would bear witness that His providential hand had planned and sketched it all. The reader can observe how the coming "end of time" is inundated with cycles of seven. (Immediately following the chart the meaning of each cycle will be discussed.)

The cornerstone or the point of origin which gave rise to the chart below was the birth of Jesus in 5 B.C. From this divine moment in history we proceeded to find the year 2000. This took us to the year of 1996. I felt that if 1996 was the beginning of Daniel's seventieth week, then surely it would intersect in cycles of seventy years with the beginning of Daniel's prophecy of seventy weeks.

What followed, therefore, was truly amazing as I discovered how so many of the important historical events began to intersect the year 1996, as well as 2003. What stirred my interest the most was when the year A.D. 29 intersected with 1996 in the seven year cycle. I think you will find the following chart very interesting and perhaps enlightening.

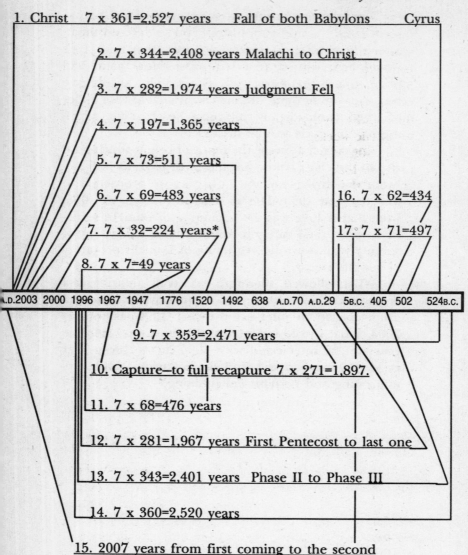

1. Christus   7 x 361=2,527 years   Fall of both Babylons   Cyrus

2. 7 x 344=2,408 years Malachi to Christ

3. 7 x 282=1,974 years Judgment Fell

4. 7 x 197=1,365 years

5. 7 x 73=511 years

6. 7 x 69=483 years

7. 7 x 32=224 years*

8. 7 x 7=49 years

16. 7 x 62=434

17. 7 x 71=497

A.D.2003 2000 1996 1967 1947   1776 1520 1492 638 A.D.70 A.D.29 5B.C. 405 502 524B.C.

9. 7 x 353=2,471 years

10. Capture—to full recapture 7 x 271=1,897.

11. 7 x 68=476 years

12. 7 x 281=1,967 years First Pentecost to last one

13. 7 x 343=2,401 years   Phase II to Phase III

14. 7 x 360=2,520 years

15. 2007 years from first coming to the second

---

*The first beast of Revelation would exist as a sovereign world power for 7 x 32=224 years until he merges into the second beast in the year 2000.

1. 524 B.C.—A.D. 2003: 7 x 361 = 2,527 years from the fall of ancient Babylon in 524 B.C. to the fall of the end-time Babylon the great in A.D. 2003. The prophet Isaiah foretold the coming of King Cyrus, who came in 524 B.C. and set the captives free. He also foretold the coming of Jesus both in Bethlehem and at the time of the end. From Cyrus to Christ's Second Coming is 361 prophetic weeks.

2. 405 B.C.—A.D. 2003: 7 x 344 = 2,408 years the prophet Malachi prophesied, "For, behold, the day cometh, that shall burn as an oven; and all the proud, yea, and all that do wickedly, shall be stubble: and the day that cometh shall burn them up, saith the Lord of hosts, that it shall leave them neither root nor branch." (Mal. 4:1) 405 B.C.—start of second phase of "the seventy weeks" until the end of the seventieth week. 344 prophetic weeks.

3. A.D. 29—A.D. 2003: 7 x 282 = 1,974 years between the time when the judgement of God fell upon Jesus, and when the judgment shall fall upon the world. When the blood of the Lamb was released, until it had completed its divine purpose. 282 prophetic weeks.

4. A.D. 638—A.D. 2003: 7 x 195 = 1,365 years from the capture of Jerusalem by the Moslem Mohammed until, the attempted capture by the beast, and the full redemption of Jerusalem from the Moslem religion. 195 prophetic weeks.

5. A.D. 1492—A.D. 2003: 7 x 73 = 511 years from the coming of Christopher Columbus to the final coming of Christ Jesus. From the opening of the New World to the opening of the new millennium. From man's noblest effort to bring freedom upon the earth, to the Son who will make the earth "free indeed." 73 prophetic weeks.

6. A.D. 1520—A.D. 2003: 7 x 69 = 483 years from the Protestant Reformation to the restitution. Martin Luther was excommunicated from Catholicism in 1520. It was

in the summer of that same year that Martin Luther brought out several great manifestos. Freed from the beast that bound him, to freedom from the beast who will bind the whole world. 69 prophetic weeks.

7. A.D. 1776—A.D. 2000: 7 x 32 = 224 years. The first beast of Revelation would exist as a sovereign world power for 224 years until he merges into the second beast in the year 2000. 32 prophetic weeks.

8. A.D. 1947—A.D. 1996: 7 x 7 = 49 years. From the rebuilding of the homeland of the Jewish people and time of their coming home. The sure sign of the end of the age of man. The fulfillment of many biblical prophecies. 7 prophetic weeks.

9. 524 B.C.—A.D. 1947: 7 x 353 = 2,471 years, approval of second beast Persia to set up Israel as a nation again in 524 B.C. to the approval of second beast, the United Nations to set up Israel again as a nation in 1947. 353 prophetic weeks.

10. A.D. 70—A.D. 1967: 7 x 271 = 1,897 years, capture of Jerusalem until Jerusalem completely recaptured (old city)—Wailing Wall set free. 271 prophetic weeks.

11. A.D. 1520—A.D. 1996: 7 x 68 = 476 years from the beginning of the Reformation, where the heralding of the gospel of the "just shall live by faith"; until the army of the Lord shall go forth, with infallible proof, revealing to the world for the last time that only by faith in Jesus will man be justified to escape the wrath to come.

12. A.D. 29—A.D. 1996: 7 x 281 = 1,967 years from the time the gospel went from Pentecost until the time of the last Pentecostal anointing, the covenant call. 281 prophetic weeks.

13. 405 B.C.—A.D. 1996: 7 x 343 = 2,401 years from the day the prophecy of Malachi was given until the day its fulfillment would begin. "In that day when I make up my jewels; . . ." 343 prophetic weeks.

14. 524 B.C.—A.D. 1996: 7 x 360 = 2,520 years from the going forth of the first phase of the seventy weeks to the going forth of the last phase. When the "good news" went out across Babylon until the "good news" goes across Babylon for the last time. 360 prophetic weeks.

15. 5 B.C.—A.D. 2003: If Jesus comes at the end of the seventieth week there will be 2,007 years from the coming of Jesus the first time to His coming back to earth the second time.

16. 405 B.C.—A.D. 29: 7 x 62 = 434 years from the last world of the Old Testament by the prophet Malachi to the beginning of the New Testament, on Passover in A.D. 29. 62 prophetic weeks.

17. 502 B.C.—5 B.C.: 7 x 71 = 497 years from the building of the last Jewish temple made by hands until the last "Jewish Temple" made without hands. 71 prophetic weeks.

18. 594 B.C.—A.D. 2003: 7 x 37 = 2,597 years. From the first captivity of Jerusalem in 594 B.C. until Jerusalem will be free at last, when her true king shall enter through the Eastern Gate will be 371 prophetic weeks. The last free king in Jerusalem which sat upon the throne of David was Jehoiakim in 594 B.C. Jehoiakim was a prophetic type of the Messiah. Jehoiakim means avenging, establishing, and resurrection of the Lord. Jesus is coming to avenge God of His enemies, establish His millennial kingdom, and to bring about the first resurrection. How important and unique that the year 594 fits into the scheme of the seventy year cycle.

A Deeper Look into the Old Testament

Abraham born	2322 B.C.
Isaac born	2222 B.C.
Jacob born	2162 B.C.
Joseph born	2071 B.C.—Jacob 91 years old
Benjamin born	2062 B.C.—Jacob 100 years old

Isaac dies	2042 B.C.—Jacob 120 years old
Sojourn in Egypt	2032 B.C.—Jacob 130 years old
Sojourn ends 430 years	1602 B.C.—Passover in Egypt
Moses dies	1562 B.C.—Wilderness 40 years
Israel enters	1562 B.C.—The Promise Land
Tribal Elders Rule	1552 B.C.—Joshua dies
Time of Judges	1541 B.C.—Judges 430 years
Prophet Samuel	1111 B.C.
Reign of Saul	1091 B.C.
Reign of David	1051 B.C.
Reign of Solomon	1011 B.C.
Temple Completed	1000 B.C.—The Presence of God

The Temple of God

1. From the finishing of the Temple of God in 1000 B.C. to when Jesus said it was finished upon the Cross in A.D. 29 was 1029 years or 3 x 7 x 7 x 7.

2. From the Temple in 1000 B.C. to the Temple of the Bride in A.D. 2003 is 3003 years or 7 x 429.

3. From the Temple in 1000 B.C. to the Command of Cyrus in 524 B.C. to build the 2nd temple was 476 years or 7 x 7 x 8.

4. From the Temple in 1000 B.C. to the founding of the Nation of Israel in 1947 was 2947 years or 7 x 421.

5. From the Temple in 1000 B.C. back to the Passover in 1602 B.C. was 602 years or 7 x 86.

6. From the Passover in Egypt in 1602 B.C. to the Passover of Jesus in A.D. 29 was 1631 years or 7 x 233.

7. From the Passover in Egypt in 1602 B.C. to when the Bride of Christ shall pass over death in A.D. 2003 is 3605 years or 7 x 515.

The Seven Year Gap

This book takes a close look at what the Christian can expect to face during this seventieth week of Daniel's prophecy. The final week will mark the last seven years before the start of the millennial reign of Christ. This seventieth week creates a gap between the sixth and seventh millennium. I believe, as was shown in chapter 1, that the six thousand years which God consigned to mankind will expire on Tishri of 1996, at the time of the Feast of the Trumpets (Rosh Hashanah). On this special day of the feast the Lord Jesus will "blow the trumpet," as it were, to enjoin those of a pure and clean heart unto the covenant "with many" as was foretold by Daniel (Dan. 9:27).

This covenant will come to those who have allowed the Holy Spirit to prepare them for this special anointing. The fire of this anointing may begin relatively small, but will vastly increase as the weeks come and go. God is saving the best anointing wine for this last great witness of the gospel to be preached into all the world (John 2:7–10).

The Messianic Covenant

"And He shall confirm the covenant with many for one week" (Dan. 9:27). The entire seventy week prophecy that Gabriel gave to Daniel focuses primarily upon the Messiah from beginning to end. The "He" in verse 27 can only be identified with the Messiah, simply because in verse 26 there are only two names mentioned. The first is the Messiah, who is the main topic of the paragraph; the second is the prince who would come and destroy Jerusalem. That was the Roman general, Titus.

Before Titus left Judea, over two million Jews lay dead. Titus did not confirm a covenant upon anyone, and certainly not with the Jews. Therefore, it leaves only the Messiah Jesus who will move at the beginning of Daniel's seventieth week to initiate the covenant with many. A thorough treatise of this covenant will be presented in greater detail in the chapter titled "The Final Offering of the Great and Last Sacrifice." The ending of the sixth millennium will mark the end of six thousand years which God allotted to man when He created Adam.

The seventieth week of Daniel will begin at that moment and will continue until the covenant witness has been finished, when the abomination which will bring on great desolation is ripe, and when the Bride of Christ is perfected and raptured. The seventh millennium will begin shortly after the destruction of the beast and his world system (Rev. 20:4).

(Some have asked, are you placing these dates in hard cement? No, but they are positively affirmed. The main concern in this book is not first with dates, as the reader will learn, but with what the Bible reveals the Bride of Christ will be experiencing during the seventieth week.)

It is incumbent upon us as Jesus is moving to establish His covenant and prepare His Bride for the great task that lies ahead (Rev. 11:3–6), that we not resist this awesome move of God but remain humble and prayerful, because pride in one's past spiritual attainments, as well as traditional experience, can create prejudice and blindness which can cause us to become critical to the point of being offended; particularly, when God's power is manifested beyond that which we may have previously experienced.

This was true of those in the days of Jesus. In this last move of God we must have our eyes wide open, lest our own judgment brings us into condemnation. The Christian will be facing two grave dangers. One, the possibility of being swept up into some "look-a-like" deception. Two, the possibility of missing the move of God. It will all depend upon the spiritual preparedness and sensitivity of the heart of the Christian. We will have to stay at the feet of Jesus in much prayer and supplication.

The seventieth week of Daniel's prophecy only becomes meaningful when we understand it within the context of the whole seventy weeks, or the 490 years, which were determined upon God's people. The revelation of the seventy weeks which was personally delivered to Daniel by the angel Gabriel was directly connected to the Babylonian captivity. The nation of Judah had been taken captive by Nebuchadnezzar in 594 B.C. Jeremiah had foretold this coming judgment several years before. He had also revealed that the captivity would last seventy years. The captivity which began in 594 B.C. ended in 524 B.C., exactly seventy years later.

Most Bible scholars have believed the captivity began on the secular date of 606-605 B.C. This date was surmised from Daniel 1:1 which reads, "In the third year of the reign of Jehoiakim king of Judah came Nebuchadnezzar king of Babylon unto Jerusalem and besieged it."

But, in Jeremiah 25:1, we read that the fourth year of Jehoiakim's reign was the first year of the reign of Nebuchadnezzar. We read, "The word that came to Jeremiah concerning all the people of Judah in the fourth year of Jehoiakim the son of Josiah king of Judah, that was the first year of Nebuchadnezzar king of Babylon." Nebuchadnezzar was barely on the throne in the third year of Jehoiakim. In the fifth year of the reign of Jehoiakim, Jeremiah says that the Word of God came unto him telling him that Nebuchadnezzar will be brought against them (Jer. 25:3-9).

There is absolutely no evidence in the Bible that Nebuchadnezzar came up to Jerusalem until the fifth year of his own reign. The fifth year of Nebuchadnezzar's reign would be the eighth year of Jehoiakim's reign. We read, "In his days Nebuchadnezzar king of Babylon came up, and Jehoiakim became his servant three years: Then he (Jehoiakim) turned and rebelled against him" (2 Kings 24:1). Jehoiakim, king of Judah, was in the eighth year of his own reign when he submitted himself to the rule of Nebuchadnezzar. This occurred in 597 B.C.

For three years Jehoiakim was a "subject king" to Nebuchadnezzar. Jehoiakim's entire reign lasted for eleven years. It was the last three years of his reign when Jehoiakim was a puppet to Babylon that Daniel is speaking of in Daniel 1:1. "In the third year of the reign of Jehoiakim king of Judah came Nebuchadnezzar king of Babylon unto Jerusalem, and besieged it." Daniel clearly identifies the time he is speaking of, when in the next verse he says, "and the Lord gave Jehoiakim king of Judah into this hand" (Dan. 1:2).

Daniel can only be speaking of the third year of Jehoiakim's reign, under Nebuchadnezzar, because there was no besieging of Jerusalem during the first eight years of Jehoiakim's reign. The third year under Nebuchadnezzar was the eleventh and final year of the reign of Jehoiakim as king of Judah. Nebuchadnezzar came that same year of 594 B.C. and besieged Jerusalem, replacing Jehoiakim with Jehoiachin, the son of Jehoiakim. Jehoiachin reigned three months and ten days when Nebuchadnezzar came against Jerusalem and besieged and took the city (2 Kings 24:10–16).

This was when the first captivity occurred. The year was 594 B.C. Jeremiah specifically agreed that the captivity began when Nebuchadnezzar carried Jeconiah (Jehoiachin) and thousands of Jews captive to Babylon (Jer. 27:20, 24:1).

The seventy year captivity prophesied by Jeremiah came upon them during the reign of Jehoiachin which began in the year 594 B.C., and would terminate under King Cyrus of Persia when he conquered Babylon exactly seventy years later.

It was just a few weeks after capturing Babylon that Cyrus issued the famous decree and some fifty thousand Jews made their way back to Jerusalem with money in hand. This prophecy of Jeremiah came to pass in

524 B.C. (A full account of this first captivity and the deportation of the captives to Babylon is recorded in 2 Kings 24:10-16.)

```
605————————8 years————————597——3 years—594
Jehoiakim's Reign                    Jehoiakim Made
    Begins                               Puppet King

Captivity                                           Captivity
Begins:                                             Ends:
594———————— 70 year captivity————————524
```

These seventy weeks of Daniel's prophecy, given to him by the angel Gabriel, are a period of 490 years of time in which God will accomplish certain things for His own glory. The 490 year prophecy is dispersed over a period of 2,527 years. The 490 prophetic years were divided into three specific segments and would manifest in three separate periods of time.

The first period covered forty-nine years, and focused upon God reestablishing "His house" upon the earth in the city of Jerusalem. These first seven weeks (forty-nine years) concluded when the walls had been built and when the city of Jerusalem had been restored. These forty-nine years (seven weeks) began in 524 B.C. and ended in 475 B.C.

The second period covered 434 years and would take up the majority of the 490 years. This phase of sixty-two prophetic weeks focused upon the coming of the Messiah. This period bridged the gap between the ending of the Old Testament as it appears in the Bible, and the beginning of the new covenant at the Cross. The Old Testament ended in the year 405 B.C. with the prophet Malachi, and exactly 434 years later in A.D. 29 the legality of the New Testament was set in force.

The third and final period is reserved until the time of the end. This final week of seven years will be the crowning moment of God's divine plan since Adam and Eve fell. This seven years will bring all that God had foretold through His prophets into a full consummation. The heart of God will be fully satisfied when death is overcome and perfection is manifested in His people. Then can come the restitution of all things (Acts 3:21). Evil will be banished from the face of the earth. All that Jesus died and paid for will be realized in the glorification of His Bride.

I believe that God has reserved these last seven years specifically for Himself. This is the reason why the seventieth week is found dividing the millenniums. This is His day, His hour, His time to make bare His holy arm unto the nations, and to fill the earth with His glory. It is the Day of the Lord!

In the beginning God created the earth in seven days. Those first years of creation lay solely in His hands. The last seven years will be no different. He will have it so in the end. God will finish the work in seven years "and cut it short in righteousness: because a short work will the Lord make upon the earth" (Rom. 9:28).

Chapter Three

The Seventy Weeks

The angel Gabriel said to Daniel, "Thou art greatly beloved" (Dan. 9:23). What an expression to have someone make to you, particularly when the one who is making it had just come from the throne of God. What we are hearing from the lips of the angel is the divine opinion that heaven had of Daniel. We hear words nearly the same, spoken to Jesus at His baptism, "This is my beloved son, in whom I am well pleased" (Matt. 3:17).

The prophet Daniel had touched heaven, by his prayer of intercession, on behalf of his people and his desire to know when the captivity of his people would end. But, Daniel long before had proven himself to God. He had become one of God's choice prophets, and had developed a very close and respected relationship with Him. No one person in the Old Testament had lived a life of more purity. We can find no testimony of another which was more dedicated to prayer. Daniel understood what his covenant afforded him, and the powerful partnership that it created between him and his God. He feared neither beast nor king.

We can see in Daniel a prophetic type of those who will be called to this end-time covenant with Jesus, and be privileged to enter into the sacrificial anointing which will be unleashed at the beginning of Daniel's seventieth week.

Daniel tells us that in the first year of the Persian king, Cyrus, Darius the Mede, said that he "understood from certain books that Jeremiah the prophet had foretold that the captivity of his people would end after seventy years." Daniel tells us upon learning this, "I set my face unto the Lord God, to seek by prayer and supplications, with fasting, and sackcloth, and ashes" (Dan. 9:3). The desired result of Daniel's great intercession was that his people be forgiven and that God would once again show mercy upon them. Mercy always follows repentance.

A letter containing one of the prophecies of Jeremiah had been sent to Babylon shortly after the first captivity in 594 B.C. (Jer. 29:1). Daniel, no doubt, was studying this very letter. He would have read the following: "For thus saith the Lord, that after seventy years be accomplished at Babylon I will visit you, and perform my good word toward you, in causing you to return to this place" (Jer. 29:10).

The seventy years of the Babylonian captivity ended with the surrender of Babylon to Cyrus, king of the Medes and Persians, in 524 B.C. Daniel tells us that it was at that time, immediately after the surrender, that he set his face unto the Lord God to seek Him on behalf of his people. Daniel in great repentance and intercession was praying that God would hearken and do and defer not (Dan. 9:19).

While Daniel was in prayer the angel Gabriel appeared to him and touched him. Gabriel then spoke, "O Daniel, I am now come forth to give thee skill and understanding" (Dan. 9:22).

Here is what Gabriel told Daniel.

> Seventy weeks are determined upon thy people and upon thy holy city, to finish the transgression, and to make an end of sins, and to make reconciliation for iniquity, and to bring in everlasting righteousness, and to seal up the vision and prophecy, and to anoint the most holy.

> Know therefore and understand that from the
> going forth of the commandment to restore
> and to build Jerusalem unto the Messiah the
> prince shall be seven weeks, and threescore and
> two weeks: the street shall be built again, and
> the wall, even in troublous times. And after
> threescore and two weeks shall Messiah be cut
> off, but not for Himself: and the people of the
> prince that shall come shall destroy the city and
> the sanctuary; and the end thereof shall be with
> a flood, and unto the end of the war desola-
> tions are determined. And he shall confirm the
> covenant with many for one week: and in the
> midst of the week he shall cause the sacrifice
> and the oblation to cease, and for the over-
> spreading of abominations he shall make it
> desolate, even until the consummation, and that
> determined shall be poured upon the desolate.
> (Dan. 9:24–27)

We have already come to understand that the seventy weeks of this prophecy was a period of time that
represented 490 years. Gabriel was careful to reveal
that the 490 years would be divided into three distinct
segments of time. The division was revealed by Gabriel
in such a way so as to enable one to understand the
number of years given to each segment, as well as, to
be able to identify the time in history when each phase
of years was to be applied.

The first was a period of seven weeks or forty-nine
years, which would begin at the time the commandment was given to build and restore Jerusalem. The
second would be a period of sixty-two weeks or 434
years, which would conclude at the death of the Messiah. The third period would be one week covering
only seven years, which would come at the "time of the
end." The angel Gabriel could not have spoken with
more clarity when he told Daniel, "Know therefore and

understand, that from the going forth of the commandment to restore and build Jerusalem" (Dan. 9:25).
This was marking the moment in time when the seventy weeks (490 years) would begin.

The Persian king, Cyrus, had been selected by God
over a century before he was even born, that he would
be God's chosen instrument to issue the commandment. We read of this choice by God, in a prophecy
given by the prophet Isaiah 190 years before God
brought Cyrus to Babylon to fulfill His will.

> Thus saith of Cyrus, He is my shepherd, and
> shall perform all my pleasure; even saying to
> Jerusalem, thou shalt be built; and to the temple,
> thy foundation shall be laid. (Isa. 44:28) Thus
> saith the Lord to His anointed, to Cyrus, whose
> right hand I have holden, . . . I have raised him
> up in righteousness, and I will direct all his
> ways; he shall build my city, and he shall let go
> my captives, not for price nor reward, saith the
> Lord of hosts. (Isa. 45:1, 13)

The Jewish historian Josephus writes that when
Cyrus took over the throne he discovered a copy of the
Book of Isaiah that prophesied his name and the things
he would do for Jerusalem. According to Josephus,
Cyrus was so stirred in his mind that he sent the fol-
lowing proclamation throughout all Asia:

> Thus saith the king: since God almighty has
> appointed me to be king of the inhabitable earth
> I believe that he is that God which the nation of
> the Israelites worship; for indeed he foretold
> my name by the prophets, and that I should
> build him a house at Jerusalem in the country
> of Judea. (*The Complete Works of Josephus*, Book
> XI [Grand Rapids, Mich.: Kregel Publications,
> 1981], 228)

Josephus continues,

> Accordingly, when Cyrus read this, and admired
> the divine power, an earnest desire and ambi-
> tion seized upon him to fulfill what was so
> written; so he called for the most eminent Jews
> that were in Babylon, and said to them, that he
> gave them leave to go back to their own coun-
> try, and to rebuild their city, Jerusalem, and the
> temple of God. (Ibid.)

We can turn to the Bible in the Book of Ezra, the
scribe, and read the personal testimony by Ezra that
Cyrus sent out such a decree throughout the whole
kingdom of Persia.

> Now in the first year of Cyrus king of Persia,
> that the word of the Lord by the mouth of
> Jeremiah might be fulfilled, the Lord stirred up
> the spirit of Cyrus king of Persia, that he made
> a proclamation throughout all His kingdom, and
> put it also in writing, saying,

> Thus saith Cyrus king of Persia, the Lord God
> of heaven hath given me all the kingdoms of
> the earth; and he hath charged me to build
> Him an house at Jerusalem, which is in Judah.

> Who is there among you of all His people? His
> God be with him, and let him go up to Jerusa-
> lem, which is in Judah, and build the house of
> the Lord God of Israel, (He is the God,) which
> is in Jerusalem.

> And whosoever remaineth in any place where
> he sojourneth, let the men of his place help him
> with silver, and with gold, and with goods, and
> with beasts, beside the freewill offering for the
> house of God that is in Jerusalem. (Ezra 1:1-4)

In light of the foregoing, no serious student is
going to look to another day and another king as the
one God chose to issue the command to build and
restore Jerusalem. God chose Cyrus, and what theolo-

gian can withstand and dispute the Word and choice
of God. Ezra was one of the main actors in the resto-
ration of Jerusalem. He most surely was convinced that
Cyrus was the appointed one to give the command. He
dedicates the first four verses of his book to that very
thing. The law under Moses taught that everything was
to be established by two or more witnesses. Cyrus is
the only king that meets that safeguard.

The commandment to restore and build Jerusalem
was decreed by Cyrus in 524 B.C. Gabriel told Daniel
that from the going forth of this command until the
Messiah, the Prince, there would be seven weeks (49
years), and threescore and two weeks (434 years). The
wording structure of Gabriel obviously reveals that the
forty-nine years and the 434 years would be two distinct periods of time which would not run consecu-
tively. The intended purpose was that Daniel, as well
as, others would understand that the division of the
time (49 years and 434 years) would reveal two separate phases, and between these two phases would be a
number of years divinely ordered which would fill the
gap. The gap would begin when the first phase of
seven weeks (49 years) ended. Cyrus gave the command in 524 B.C. Therefore, the gap would begin forty-
nine years later in 475 B.C.

In the third year of Cyrus, three years after the
commandment was issued, Daniel writes that he came
to understand the vision of the seventy weeks, and that
the time appointed was long (Dan. 10:1). Yes, it would
be long, for the vision of the seventy weeks from start
to finish would cover a period of 2,527 years, or thirty-
six cycles of seventy years, plus seven years. The 36
cycles of 70 or 2,520 years would begin at the commandment in 524 B.C. and would extend to the end of
the six thousand years given to man.

524 B.C. ——————— 2527 years ——————— 2003
5 cycles of 490 years + 70 + 7

I believe the first year of Daniel's seventieth week will begin on the first day of the Jewish new year which begins on September 1996. This date on the Lord's calendar would be two thousand years from the time Jesus was born. The final seven years of the seventieth week will extend to the year 2003, with Armageddon beginning sometime in 2004. The "Lord's Calendar" begins in the fall instead of January 1 or, on the eighth day, or sometime in the eighth year after the ending of the year 2000. This will be the first year of the seventh millennium. The reign of Christ upon the earth will immediately follow Armageddon.

For the Word of God to remain prophetically consistent the last seven years of Daniel's prophecy, it would have to be systematically enjoined into the overall network of God's "blueprint" of time.

Gabriel tells us that the Messiah would be cut off or crucified at the conclusion of the second phase of sixty-two weeks or 434 years. The meaning of the Messiah being "cut off" is clearly established by the prophet Isaiah some 190 years prior to Cyrus's command in 524 B.C.

> He was taken from prison and from judgment: and who shall declare his generation? For he was "cut off" out of the land of the living: for the transgression of my people was he stricken. And he made his grave with the wicked, and with the rich in his death; because he had done no violence, neither was any deceit in his mouth. (Isa. 53:8, 9)

Jesus was crucified or "cut off" out of the land of the living at the time of the Passover in A.D. 29. Daniel reveals that the second phase of 434 years would extend unbroken to the time the Messiah was "cut off."

If we subtract the 434 years from A.D. 29 it will bring us back to the year of 405 B.C. The date would mark when the second phase of the sixty-two weeks

(434 years) would begin. I believe that the starting time was, also, on the Jewish new year of 405 B.C.

The command of Cyrus was given in 524 B.C., and at that command the first phase of the seventy weeks began. The first phase would last for seven weeks or forty-nine years. If we subtract forty-nine years from 524 B.C. it will take us to the year of 475 B.C. We can see that the time which lapses between the ending of the first phase in 475 B.C. and the beginning of the second phase which is 405 B.C. is a period of seventy years (475–405 = 70). This would be consistent with the whole pattern God had predesigned.

```
         Phase I                              Phase II
           49                    70              434
524─────────475─────────Gap──────405─────────A.D. 29
         7 x 7              7 x 10          7 x 62
```

The above graph shows us that the first two phases of Daniel's prophecy covers a period of 483 years with a gap of seventy years between them. The 483 years took up sixty-nine of the seventy weeks. One week or a period of seven years remains to be fulfilled. The last or seventieth week was to occur at the time of the end. We learned in chapter 1 that the time of the end is a seven year period which will begin in the fall of 1996, and will conclude in the fall of 2003. This seven year period is the seventieth week of Daniel's prophecy. The following graph will illustrate:

```
        1,967 Years or 281 Cycles of 7        7
A.D. 29 ─────────────────────────── 1996──────2003
```

From the ending of the second phase in A.D. 29 to the ending of the third phase in 2003 there are 1,974 years or 282 cycles of seven.

The year 524 B.C. is without question one of the most important dates in Bible history. It reveals a year in history chosen by God when on His "blueprint" of time He would begin to unfold His "prophetic mystery" of the "time of the end," as well as, to establish the date when His Son would break the curse of Satan's power, and open the stream of living water into the world.

524 B.C. would be one of the most important years in Bible prophecy.

1. Three prophecies of Daniel would be fulfilled (chapters 2, 5, 9).

2. The prophecy given by Jeremiah of the ending of the Babylonian captivity would be fulfilled.

3. Isaiah's prophecy of Cyrus and his calling of God to give the command as revealed to Daniel by Gabriel would be fulfilled.

4. Not only was Daniel on the scene at this time, but God had Ezra, Nehemiah, Haggai, Zerrubbabel, Zechariah and Iddo the Prophet, along with a host of other zealous servants. It may well be the only time in the history of the Old Testament that God assembled such an extensive host of His servants and prophets to fulfill His Word and execute His bidding.

5. God sent the angel Gabriel to light the way.

6. The kingdom of Babylon fell, which is a type of the end-time Babylon (Rev. 18:2).

7. The Second Temple of God began to be built and the return of the Jews to their homeland. Symbolic of the end-time, the temple of the Holy Ghost and the gathering of the elect.

8. The rise of the second beast (bear)—Persia (Dan. 7:5). Symbolic of the rise of the second beast at the "end of the world." Persia in the beginning helped Israel to become reestablished in their homeland as the second beast has done for Israel in these last days.

The fact that the embarking of the seventy week prophecy of Daniel was sealed by a great cloud of witnesses is evidence enough that God, Himself, had stamped that divine moment in time with the finger prints of His own hand. Whether the dates of secular history ever agree with the calendar of God makes no difference. For, the wisdom of man is foolishness unto God, and anytime we attempt to utilize secular dates to interpret God's prophetic table of time, we will usually always miss the mark.

The prophet Isaiah has told us,

> For my thoughts are not your thoughts, neither are your ways my ways, saith the Lord. For as the heavens are higher than the earth, so are my ways higher than your ways, and my thoughts than your thoughts. (Isa. 55: 8–9)

> For the wisdom of this world is foolishness with God. For it is written, He taketh the wise in their own craftiness. (1 Cor. 3:19)

Chapter Four

The First Phase of the Seventy Weeks

Seven Weeks—Forty-nine Years

The decree of the Persian King Cyrus, which fulfilled the commandment given by the angel Gabriel, was issued sometime in the year 524 B.C. Within a matter of weeks over fifty thousand Jews (including children) made their way back to their homeland. There were among this vast number of people many of the "ancients" who had been taken captive seventy years earlier by King Nebuchadnezzar. One of these was Ezra's father, Seraiah. He was one of the chief priests who had served in Solomon's temple before it was destroyed by the Babylonian king in 583 B.C.

The jubilant hour had come and the sure word of prophecy had been fulfilled, the faithful were heading back to Zion with songs of everlasting joy. It was going to take men and women of the strongest faith to look upon the ruins of their beloved city and have the heart and soul to believe that she could live again. Many of these were taken captive before the destruction of their city, Jerusalem, and had never witnessed the carnage.

But, the joy of the Lord was their strength; the very words of one of their prophet leaders, Nehemiah, whom God anointed simply because he had a heart that could weep over Jerusalem and a mind that was willing to work.

This was the mind and heart of many of those who
made the first pilgrimage back to Jerusalem in 524 B.C.
We see this in the Book of Ezra. These words were
written when the foundation of the temple was laid. By
reading these words it will give us an appreciation of
the deep feeling they carried within their hearts. Let us
go back to that day in ancient Jerusalem.

> And when the builders laid the foundation of
> the temple of the Lord, they set the priests in
> their apparel with trumpets, and the Levites the
> sons of Asaph with cymbals, to praise the Lord,
> after the ordinance of David king of Israel.
>
> And they sang together by course in praising
> and giving thanks unto the Lord; because He is
> good, for His mercy endureth forever toward
> Israel. And all the people shouted with a great
> shout, when they praised the Lord, because the
> foundation of the house of the Lord was laid.
>
> But many of the priests and Levites and chief of
> the fathers, who were ancient men, that had
> seen the first house, when the foundation of
> this house laid before their eyes, wept with a
> loud voice; and many shouted with joy:
>
> So that the people could not discern the noise
> of the shout of joy from the noise of the weep-
> ing of the people: for the people shouted with
> a loud shout and the noise was heard afar off.
> (Ezra 3:10–13)

When the people of God begin to make a noise in
the land, the devil can't stand it and immediately begins an assault. This attack began at the end of the
second year in 522 B.C. This attack was so powerful and
well organized that Ezra tells us, "Then the people of
the land weakened the hands of the people of Judah,
and troubled them in building, and hired counsellors
against them, to frustrate their purpose, all the days of

Cyrus" (Ezra 4:4-5), which would be for the next seven years.

This warfare against God's people would intensify under the next Persian king, Cambysus (called Artaexerxes), to the extent that this king would issue an order that all construction cease, including the city. God gave Cambysus seven years in which to repent. Although he was the son of Cyrus, he did things which were evil in the sight of God, and God removed him from the throne. This was in the year 508 B.C.

Later in that year God raised up a king by the name of Daris Hystaspes. It was about this same time that God called forth prophets to strengthen and encourage His people. These prophets were Haggai and Zechariah. Both prophets would make a contribution to the Old Testament.

The enemies of Israel would make an attempt to control the mind of King Darius, but the Jews by the direction of the prophets, no doubt, sent emissaries to Darius, whereupon he made a search of the records in Babylon. There he found the decree of Cyrus. This occurred in the second year of his reign in 506 B.C. Darius upon reading the decree of Cyrus, sent out his own decree, which said in no uncertain terms that the hindering cease and "that of the king's goods, even of the tribute beyond the river, forthwith expenses be given unto these men" (Ezra 6:8).

The work upon the city and the temple were renewed with great vigor. "And this house was finished on the third day of the month Adar, which was in the sixth year of the reign of Darius the king" (Ezra 6:15).

This tells us that the temple was completed in the year 502 B.C. That date is very interesting, because, from the time that this temple was completed until the time of the birth of God's temple, Jesus, in 5 B.C., there was a period of 497 years, or seven times seventy-one.

502 B.C. ————————— 7 x 71 ————————— 5 B.C.

God knew that those attacks which had been made upon Israel were legal because there was serious sin in the camp. But, since the temple had now been completed, God wanted to restore a full understanding and purification of the law and ordinance to His house. Therefore, one year later in 501 B.C. God sent Ezra, who was greatly qualified, to Jerusalem and anointed him in teaching and interpreting the law of God.

Many Bible teachers have taught that Ezra went up to Jerusalem in 458 B.C., but what these teachers overlook is that Ezra's father, Seraiah, was a chief priest in Jerusalem back in 583 B.C., and that Ezra himself wrote that he was living in Babylon thirty years after the destruction of his city (2 Esd. 3:1, Apocrypha). This would have been in 553 B.C.

Since Seraiah, Ezra's father (Ezra 7:1) had a son Jozadak who was old enough to be recorded in the Babylonian captivity, surely we must assume that Ezra must have been born around 575 B.C. (1 Chron. 6: 14, 15). If Ezra went to Jerusalem to begin his ministry in 458 B.C., then he would have been 117 years of age when he began his priestly ministry in Jerusalem. Not to mention, that his father, Seraiah, was there and was recognized as one of the chief rulers when Nehemiah arrived thirteen years later (Neh. 11:4, 11). Also, he is mentioned in Nehemiah 10:1-2. Seraiah by this time would be approaching 168 years of age. The Bible says come let us reason together. It is not reasonable for Ezra or Nehemiah (who came to Jerusalem in 488 B.C.), to have come to Jerusalem under any other king except Darius Hystaspes.

I do know that some of the Bible teachers have chosen the later date for Ezra and Nehemiah simply because the Bible says in both their books that they came up to Jerusalem under a king called Artaxerxes.

But, Artaxerxes is a name for a race of Persian kings according to William Smith LL.D., New Standard Reference Bible. There are great portions of the books of Ezra and Nehemiah which are written in the third person. Therefore the use of Arataxerxes in describing the Persian monarch reigning at that particular time no doubt reflected the writer's personal idiom.

The second king of Persia, Cambyses, was called Artaxerxes. It was an accepted tradition to refer to a Persian king by a distinctive title at times, instead of using his name. We see this being done with Cyrus both in Daniel and again in Ezra. He is called Cyrus in Ezra 4:5, and in verse 6 he is called Ahasurerus. The husband of Esther was called Ahasuerus. Some Bible scholars believe that Esther was married to Darius, some to Xerxes, and some to Cyrus (the son of Xerxes), who was called by the Greeks, Artaxerxes.

If we study the genealogy of Mordecai carefully we see that his grandfather Kish came over in the Babylonian Captivity, and Mordecai and Esther were of the same generation. Therefore, Esther was either the wife of Darius or Xerxes but not of Cyrus (Artaxerxes Longimanus) as so many have conjectured.

The problem of identification is not the only problem one has with Persian history. There is a serious problem of establishing the exact length of some of the king's reigns. Some scholars confuse the twelve-year reign of Xerxes I in Babylon with his twenty-year reign in Persepolis and Susa. During his reign in Babylon, his father Darius was on the throne over all the Persian Empire. Under the entry entitled "Xerxes I," the 15th edition of the Encyclopaedia Britannica states that Xerxes I's reign lasted twenty-one years, while Josephus tells us that this same Xerxes I, son of Hystaspes, reigned for at least twenty-nine years (*The Complete Works of Josephus* [Grand Rapids, Mich.: Kregel Publications, 1981], 237).

It is difficult to establish ancient dates with any degree of accuracy past the time of Alexander the Great in 330 B.C. As you have probably already noticed, the author's date for the beginning of the Babylonian Captivity (594 B.C.) is approximately three to four years nearer than most secular dates. It is the author's opinion that Persian history could be overextended by as much as twelve to fifteen years. The Bible reveals that the Babylonian Captivity began when Jechoiachin was removed from the throne by Nebuchadnezzar in 594 B.C. The captivity lasted seventy years. This brings us to the year 524 B.C. when it ended. Secular scholars say that Babylon fell in 536 B.C., 537 B.C., 538 B.C., 539 B.C., and most Bible scholars have considered those dates fairly accurate. But, as was earlier shown, the Babylonian Captivity occurred three months and ten days after the removal of Jehoiakim, and not in the third year of his eleven year reign. This of itself takes eight years off the length of the Persian Empire according to secular chronology. Therefore, from the Bible we can see that the secular chronology of Persia is overextended.

Nehemiah left Susa, where he was the king's cupbearer, and came to Jerusalem thirteen years after Ezra in 488 B.C. He became governor, perhaps relieving the aging Zerrubabbel, and would labor exceedingly hard, even with his own hands in helping build the walls and restore the city. We see that he and Ezra were there together for part of his governorship (Neh. 8:9). Nehemiah's duties would run to the end of the first seven prophetic weeks (7 x 7) or the first period of forty-nine years.

We read that after twelve years he goes up to Babylon in the thirty-second year reign of the Persian king. He returns and further puts all things in order. I personally believe that when that was accomplished, the first prophetic segment of forty-nine years expired. Let's look at the first forty-nine years on the following graph.

524————————————502—501—————488——475

502 temple completed, 501 Ezra goes to Jerusalem, 488 Nehemiah goes to Jerusalem.

The completion of the first seven weeks of Daniel's prophecy took place in 475 B.C. The closing of the Book of Nehemiah marks its conclusion. The angel Gabriel did not convey to Daniel the number of years which would separate the ending of the first seven week phase and the beginning of the second phase which would last for sixty-two weeks or 434 years. The second phase would be heralded by the ending of the Old Testament. The prophet that God chose to speak His final word, which would seal up the law and bind up the testimony of the Old Testament, was Malachi.

This would occur in the year 405 B.C. The year 405 B.C. was determined by subtracting the sixty-two weeks or 434 years from the crucifixion of Christ in A.D. 29. The gap between phase one and phase two would turn out to be exactly seventy years. From the date of 405 B.C., sixty-two prophetic weeks or 434 years later, Gabriel told Daniel that the Messiah would be "cut off" or crucified.

There is one truly amazing observation about this period of time. This has to do with John the Baptist. We find Malachi in 405 B.C. giving this prophecy, "Behold, I will send my messenger, and he shall prepare the way before me: and the Lord, whom ye seek, shall suddenly come to his temple, even the messenger of the covenant, whom ye delight in: Behold, he shall come, saith the Lord of Hosts" (Mal. 3:1). Over four centuries later, Jesus speaking of John the Baptist says, "Verily I say unto you, among them that are born of women there hath not risen a greater than John the Baptist. . . . And if ye will receive it, this is Elias, which was for to come" (Matt. 11:11, 14).

We read in the first verse of the Gospel of Mark, "The beginning of the Gospel of Jesus Christ, the Son of God; As it is written in the prophets, behold, I send my messenger before thy face, which shall prepare thy way before thee" (Mark 1:1-2). The Old Testament is concluded with a prophecy of John the Baptist, and the New Testament is opened by the ministry of the prophet John the Baptist. The observation is, from the sojourn of Israel in Egypt until the night of the Passover, there was a period of 430 years of spiritual darkness.

We see in like parallel that from the ending of the old covenant prophets in 405 B.C. to that moment when John the Baptist, on the banks of Jordan River by the spirit of God, proclaimed before the great host of Jews exactly 430 years later, "Behold the Lamb of God who taketh away the sins of the world."

From the blood of the old covenant to the blood of the New Testament, even though that blood was yet in the veins of the Lamb, John sensed its great purifying presence as he turned to Jesus and said, "I have need to be baptized of thee." The proclamation made by John, "Behold the Lamb," in conjunction with the baptism of Jesus both by water and by the spirit inaugurated His ministry. This was in the month of Tishri (September), A.D. 25, exactly 430 years after the ending of the Old Testament. Malachi, also, said, "The Lord, whom ye seek, shall suddenly come to His temple" (Mal. 3:1). This Jesus did: 430 years later He comes as "refiners fire" and "Fuller's soap" (a good description of the blood of Jesus).

Dear reader, is God a god who has measured carefully the years of time and written them in a book, which we know as the sure word of prophecy? Yes, He is and has!

In these first chapters we have attempted to show God's personal involvement in history, and the eye of His scrutiny which the prophets have at times revealed.

The angel Gabriel was sent to open the beginning of the seventy weeks, and now as we are approaching the seventieth and final week, how sobering is the thought of who our God shall send to commence this last great consummation of time. There is little doubt that it will be Gabriel whom God shall send, since it was he that oversaw the revelation.

The Apostle John witnessed this final throwing of the gospel net into the sea for the souls of men. "And I saw another angel fly in the midst of heaven, having the everlasting Gospel to preach unto them that dwell on the earth, and to every nation, and kindred, and tongue, and people, Saying with a loud voice, fear God, and give glory to Him; for the hour of His judgment is come: and worship Him that made heaven, and earth, and the sea, and the fountains of waters" (Rev. 14:6–7).

I believe that the above vision of John is that special end-time anointing which God shall give unto the faithful, which will reap God's vineyard for the final time. The loud voice is representative of the mighty power and great authority by which the word will go forth. This angel message can be none other than the long prophesied covenant which the Messiah would confirm with many, which Daniel foretold (Dan. 9:27). How important it is that God's people are ready and prepared for that special hour of God's visitation. May the Lord find His servants ready, waiting and willing when He shall call.

For as a Snare Shall It Come

Almost two thousand years ago Jesus warned the world that a day would come, when a great and awful snare would be laid for all who dwell upon the earth. This snare, according to Jesus, would be implemented at the time when the fig tree (Israel) was being birthed, and that it would occur in that generation.

> Behold the fig tree, and all the trees; when they now shoot forth, ye see and know of your own selves that summer is now nigh at hand. So likewise ye, when ye see these things come to pass, know ye that the kingdom of God is nigh at hand. Verily I say unto you, this generation shall not pass away, till all be fulfilled. (Luke 21:29–32)

Jesus greatly amplifies this last generation in the twenty-fourth chapter of Matthew. There He alerts our attention to the prophet Daniel and the seventieth week. That very portion which Jesus was making reference reads as follows: "And for the overspreading of abominations . . . even until the consummation, and that determined shall be poured upon the desolate" (Dan. 9:27).

Here is what Jesus had to say to those who would be living in that generation when Israel would be established as a nation:

> And take heed to yourselves, lest at any time
> your hearts be overcharged with surfeiting, and
> drunkenness, and cares of this life, and so that
> day come upon you unawares.
>
> For as a snare shall it come on all them that
> dwell on the face of the whole earth.
>
> Watch ye therefore, and pray always, that ye
> may be accounted worthy to escape all these
> things that shall come to pass, and to stand
> before the Son of man. (Luke 21:34–36)

The devil told Jesus that the kingdoms of this world
belonged to him [Satan] (Matt. 4:8–9). We, as Christians, have often forgotten this truth and have looked
upon our nation more as a kingdom of God rather
than a kingdom of the world. Many times we have
been willing to blindly support and lift up the desires
of our country's presidents as if they were edicts from
heaven. Fortunately, in recent years many Christians
have awakened, and are realizing the extent to which
they have been intentionally misinformed. There are
an increasing number of Christians which are beginning to comprehend the encompassing web of deception that is at work in the shadows of our government.

John saw that to a great nation the dragon (Satan)
would give his power, his seat, and great authority
(Rev. 13:2). Daniel said that this nation-beast would
wear out the saints of God and would make war against
them. The design of Satan has been to exalt the heart
of man and stimulate his soul to crave the pleasures
and life style so highly promoted and magnified in this
present generation.

Satan knew that once Christians began to enjoy the
taste of the carnal and established their minds to so
seek for its promised delight, then the Christian would
be ripe for the slaughter. Satan's society took the man
to war, put the woman to work, divided the home,

replaced the family altar with the television, and it wasn't long until the sins of the parents had set the children's teeth on edge. It appears that most Christians did not pray their way through the "temptation" of the hour, but just gave in to the pressures and did what seemed right for them to do. Isn't that the way the world does business? Walking by sight and not by faith! Look back to the warning of Jesus, "Watch ye therefore, and pray always." For what? Watch that you do not act like or think like those who are in the world. Pray that we faint not, that our faith will not surrender nor compromise with the overpowering spirit of temptation which Satan has instilled into this generation.

Those who took the warning lightly saw their children being swept away into the cunning snares of Satan's fun and games of excitement and pleasure. Today, America is on a party binge unparalleled in the history of our nation. There is no time for the retaining of God in the thoughts of this generation. The Apostle Paul wrote of a time exactly like this:

> And even as they did not like to retain God in their knowledge, God gave them over to a reprobate mind, to do those things which are not convenient; Being filled with all unrighteousness, fornication, wickedness, covetousness, maliciousness, full of envy, murder, debate, deceit, malignity; whisperers, backbiters, haters of God, despiteful, proud, boasters, inventors of evil things, disobedient to parents. (Rom. 1:28-30)

A preacher said one time, "I have learned to just grit my teeth and bear it." Sin has always in the end caused gnashing of teeth. Jesus warned us, but few have heeded. "And seek not ye what ye shall eat, or what ye shall drink, neither be ye of doubtful mind. For all these things do the nations of the world seek after" (Luke 12:29-30). In Matthew 6:33, Jesus further counseled us: "But seek ye first the kingdom of God, and all these things shall be added unto you." The kingdom of God provides us with God's power, wisdom and love; the ingredients by which the believer can overcome the world about him.

Today, many Christians are not following the way of the kingdom, but are seeking to do the adding themselves, and it continues to take its heavy toll. The carnal desire to possess and partake of as many of the world's "things" that money can buy or find pleasure in, has caused us to become more of a lover of mammon, than a lover of God. In the process we have left the wounded strewn along the highway of modern life and brought upon ourselves the curse of spiritual destitution. Few, if any, were ever giving it a thought that they were becoming lovers of pleasure more than lovers of God. Satan, in this last generation, has glorified our society. He has held it out before us and said, "Come, eat, drink, and be merry, enjoy the good life." Before long the Christian was walking in darkness at noonday and knew it not.

Jesus foresaw the awesome temptation which Satan would use to ensnare the world at the time of the end, and prophetically pleaded, "And take heed to yourselves, lest at any time your hearts be overcharged (burdened—grievous) with surfeiting, and drunkenness, and cares of this life, and so that day come upon you unawares" (Luke 21:34).

Jesus is saying that the focus and attention of our minds can be upon the cares of this life, and by that one thing we can become blinded to what is really taking place about us, as well as, in us. "For as a snare shall it come on all them that dwell on the face of the whole earth" (Luke 21:35). Look at this Scripture! The snare would come upon all.

Daniel said that the beast would wear out the saints. Everyone is coming face to face with the wine of Satan's glittering lie. This lie will be the most seductive deception, apparently of such a necessity, that the deception will appeal to the best reasoning of man. To our natural mind it will appear to be the only right thing to do.

The word *snare* means stratagem, temptation or to trick. Satan has led the world and most Christians to become so attached to and dependent upon society, that society has ensnared them. John warns us in Revelation 3:10 that if we have kept the word of God's patience then God can keep us from this hour of the devil's strategeous temptation. Watch the truth of this wisdom which John has provided us with. When the Christian is wrapped up into the life of the world society, and at the same time becomes solely dependent upon it, he then is in a very great danger of being spiritually "worn out" and overcome.

The Apostle John was told, by the angel, that at the time of the beast the saints must exercise faith and patience (Rev. 13:10). Only patience keeps us from running ahead of God. Isn't it interesting that we are witnessing a generation of the most impatient people the world has ever seen. We are in full steam with a society which "can't wait," "gotta get it," "gotta run," and "gotta go!" This is exactly the kind of mindset that the devil is preparing wherein he will spring his trap. Apostle Paul states, "For ye have need of patience, that, after ye have done the will of God, ye might receive the promise" (Heb. 10:36). In Hebrews 6:12 we read, "Be . . . followers of them who through faith and patience inherit the promises."

Our society has led people into such a high pitch of frenzy that only a very few have learned the gospel art to be still and know that "I Am God," to know that God is a God of the now, a God of the present need, as well as, a God of the future, whatever the demand might be. The prophet Isaiah understood the great spiritual truth centuries ago: "But they that wait upon the Lord shall renew their strength; they shall mount up with wings as eagles; they shall run, and not be weary; and they shall walk, and not faint" (Isa. 40:31).

To wait before the Lord we must slow the mind down, it must cease to be overactive. For the mind to receive from God, through His spirit, the mind needs to be subject to the spirit. This can only be accomplished through prayer, fasting, and coming into God's presence through worship and meditation upon His Word, where our faith can patiently draw upon the reality of God's word of promise.

What is your day like, dear Christian? The old songs imparted great wisdom to us. "Take time to be holy, speak oft with the Lord." "Are you weak and heavy laden cumbered with a load of care, . . . take it to the Lord in prayer."

The deceptiveness of the "old man" which the apostle warns of, can easily lead one from the narrow pathway of the "simplicity which is in Jesus" into a carnal "do it yourself" religion. "But I fear, lest by any means, as the serpent beguiled Eve through his subtlety, so your minds should be corrupted from the simplicity that is in Christ" (2 Cor. 11:3). Jesus said that without Him we can do nothing. Satan is using the world to separate the believer from his love for Jesus and his hunger for the things of God. Jesus speaking of the end of the world said, "And because iniquity shall abound the love of many shall wax cold, but he that shall endure unto the end, the same shall be saved" (Matt. 24:12–13).

There is a counterfeit religion steamrolling through society today, known as the "New Age." Many Christians feel that they are exempt from this New Age movement which has made its way into all of society. It is popular because sinners can dwell there. Their primary thesis being, "I'm O.K., you're O.K.," and all each one needs to do is to tap into his own inner divine ability, and search out those wondrous powers concealed within.

This doctrine is 100 percent self-centered. Self bows before itself confessing no need for a saviour. The unregenerated are already in the grasp of the evil one, and just a little religious seeking after those "higher self powers" will prepare the seeker for a special anointing from the god of this world. Today, millions are blindly walking into this lie of the ages and unless delivered will be doomed for an eternity.

The prophet Isaiah foretold the coming of a religion from the East that we would embrace. He goes on to prophesy that we would become extremely prideful with our personal achievements. From the Amplified Bible we read that prophecy.

> Surely (Lord) you have rejected and forsaken your people, the house of Jacob, because they are filled with customs from the east and with soothsayers who foretell like the Philistines; also they strike hands and make pledges and agreements with the children of aliens.

> Their land also is full of silver and gold, neither is there any end of their treasures; their land is also full of horses, neither is there any end to their chariots.

> Their land also is full of idols; they worship the work of their own hands, what their own fingers have made. (Isa. 2:6–8)

> The Apostle Paul warned the saints at Galatia of exactly the same problem. "O foolish Galations, who hath bewitched you, that ye should not obey the truth, . . . are ye so foolish? Having begun in the spirit, are ye now made perfect by the flesh?" (Gal. 3:1–3)

Today, because of the influence of our society most Christians have become highly developed in "leaning unto their own wisdom and depending upon their own understanding." They feel little need for Jesus. Many have lost sight of Him as the supplier of their needs and the joy "filler" of their soul. I run into very few Christians who enjoy the "blessed peace" of knowing that the Lord is directing the course of their lives and who are eager to tell about it.

But, what we do hear in the Christian community are the plans believers have made and have set for themselves to attain, with little or no thought as to whether it is God's will for them. This is true, also, among the college-age people. I have listened to many high school graduates planning to enroll in some university, individuals entering into business, men and women giving little thought to marriage, and individuals taking another job because of more money, without any concern at all whether God agreed with them or not. It was what the flesh desired to do and that was all that mattered.

How careless we have become in this generation. We are doing many things without prayerful consideration. Many Christians are pretty much in the same boat as the New Agers: they have become a god unto themselves. In all their ways they acknowledge themselves and direct their own paths (Prov. 3:5). Rather than manifesting a spirit of great dependence and surrender unto the Lord's spirit, we see a spirit of independence. This spirit has been garnered from the world through education, and spawned from prideful hearts which have taken the glory for all of their accomplishments in this generation.

Most Christians have fallen prey to the philosophy that to out-smart the world, we have got to be smarter than the world. That is hardly the testimony of the prophet Daniel. We learn from Scripture that in Daniel's words, they were ten times smarter than the Babylonians, because they ate not of the king's portion, but ate from the counsel of God's Word: The

Scriptures have warned us about Babylon, the world around us. We have had this word all our Christian lives, but haven't been able to discern its truth as it relates to ourselves. Did you know that the United States was the "linen capital" of the world, particularly New York City, as well as, the financial center of the world? Isn't it interesting to read. ". . . Alas, Alas, that great city, that was clothed in fine linen, . . . and decked with gold, and precious stones, and pearls" (Rev. 18:16). To further enlarge the apostle's description of this great end-time nation-city, "For all nations have drunk of the wine of the wrath of her fornication, and the kings of the earth have committed fornication with her, and the merchants of the earth are waxed rich through the abundance of her delicacies" (Rev. 18:3).

At one time New York City was by far the largest seaport in the world. I do not believe that the actual wealth of America can now be accurately measured by man: it is too far into the trillions of dollars. But, its debt can be measured, as well as, its sins. Babylon's was (Dan. 5:25-30).

Again in Revelation 18:7 there is little doubt that John is speaking of the United States. "How much she hath glorified herself, and lived deliciously, so much torment and sorrow give her: For she saith in her heart, I sit a queen, and am no widow, and shall see no sorrow." In the midst of describing the great end-time Babylon, God speaks to His people very plainly. He tells us to, "Come out of her, my people, that ye be not partakers of her sins, and that ye receive not of her plagues" (Rev. 18:4).

The saints of God who are presently obeying the voice of God and are coming out of Babylon, are being prepared to abide in the "new and deeper covenant" of God's power and grace for these last days. These saints are no longer sipping on the wine of Babylon's society, but on the wine being served in the presence of God.

Today, all across this land Christians are spending two to six hours worshipping before one of the "images of the beast," being spiritually worn-out and deceived. Millions of Christians have joined with the world in parading weekly, if not daily, into the idolatrous video dens of Satan to indulge in those things which as Eve would say, "Are pleasant to the eyes"; again without thought of the drugging poison that is entering their soul.

I do not find John mentioning this image of television, yet, television has become the number one tool of Satan in propagandizing his life style and controlling influence throughout the earth. Who would have ever thought seventy-five years ago that one object could become the "carrier vulture" for so much evil and become an instrument for the intoxication of the minds of both the young and old, the bond and free throughout the entire world. The prophet Daniel, given the understanding from the angel Gabriel, called it the "overspreading of abominations."

Television certainly has a mouth that is speaking great things and blasphemies. It most certainly is wearing out the saints of God. As Daniel prophesied, "And he shall speak great words against the most high, and shall wear out the saints of the most high, and think to change times and laws: and they shall be given into his hand until a time and times and the dividing of time" (Dan. 7:25). Maybe the television is just the beginning of the great temptation. But it is a sinister tool, that very few realize, that is slowly softening them up for the kill.

The filth, ungodly pictures and information which is passing through the eyes into the soul of man through this medium is frightening. Yet, so many Christians are in such a stupor and are so drugged by its effect that they cannot, for one evening, pull themselves away from the "worship of this image."

The television has become the number one means of spreading fear, hate, greed, perversion, despair and murder. But, it also has become the most effective way to brainwash, manipulate and control the minds of even the most educated. I believe that in the near future this "image of the beast" will be utilized, to extremes never thought of, to promote the gospel of the anti-Christ in ways that only the spiritually discerning will detect. There is no question that television has become the beast's number one means, whereby he is intoxicating the world with the wine of his fornication.

It is true in our present world society that drugs have overspread the world and continue to increase. Crime, murder and violence are a part of every community, small or large. So is abortion—murder. Divorce has become a very accepted part of the modern lifestyle. Only 50 percent of the children in America have a home with two parents. Education has become polluted and twisted, and under the beast's control. Our children's minds are being taught the abominations of this world. Religious deception is everywhere. A spirit of confusion has entered the entire Christian world as never before. Confusion will always breed compromise with the world, whether it be doctrines or morals.

Everywhere you can hear, it doesn't really matter what you believe, just as long as you believe in Jesus. In this mindset lies the greatest deception of all. To separate Jesus from His Word is to create a Jesus of our own making. We should never forget that Jesus said, "Not every one that saith unto me, Lord, Lord, shall enter into the kingdom of heaven; but he that doeth the will of my father which is in heaven." The Apostle John put it another way in 2 John 9: "Whosoever transgresseth, and abideth not in the doctrine of Christ, hath not God. He that abideth in the doctrine of Christ, he hath both the father and the son." Jesus cannot be a personal savior to any man apart from understanding and abiding in the truth of the gospel.

If there is one sure warning trumpet that the beast is stretching the wings of his dominion, it is the undeniable evidence of the "overspreading of abomination" spoken of by the prophet Daniel. If any Christian has any question as to the authenticity of Daniel's revelation, let us not forget that Jesus pointed to it as one of the signs of the end "When ye therefore shall see the abomination of desolation, spoken of by Daniel the prophet, stand in the holy place, (Whoso readeth, let him understand)" (Matt. 24:15). (It is true that Antiochanus Ephipnnes placed a statue of Zeus in the Jewish temple in Jerusalem for all Jews to worship as God, but Jesus is certainly speaking of far wider implications.)

The whole earth is at this hour overspread with abominations. The world is falling fast into the snare of desolation. It is time to flee the world at all cost. "Come totally out of the world's life style and be separate." Do not gamble with your money, and neither with your soul. The spirit that is in the world will overcome every Christian who seeks its pleasures, no matter how harmless they appear.

The Apostle Paul put it this way, "Wherefore if ye be dead with Christ from the rudiments of the world, why, as though living in the world, are ye subject to ordinances, touch not; taste not; handle not; which all are to perish with the using; after the commandments and doctrines of men?" (Col. 2:20–22). The Apostle James warns us also, "The friendship of the world is enmity with God? Whosoever therefore will be a friend of the world is the enemy of God" (James 4:4).

Therefore, with the overspreading of the abominations the Lord is telling us to flee the wrath, to come and find shelter in the sanctuary of His holiness. Jesus, speaking to the Church, may literally be saying that we need to get far out of society, even if it be in the mountains; but for sure the implication is that if we are going to escape, we will have to flee the habits, the ways, and the sins.

We must flee the pleasure-filled life of this end-time snare of the devil. Most of all, we must flee the religious deception and the false teachers and preachers who have spurned the pure Word of the Bible and teach a gospel which is mixing the flesh with the Spirit.

As Babylon falls deeper and deeper into darkness and degradation, millions of Christians are giving less thought as to the powerful grasp Babylon has on their own souls. The spirit of the age is so strong on them, that to interfere with their present lifestyle, is not only offensive, but many will quickly remind you that you are not their judge. Most preachers have compromised and have all but given up on confronting this deeply self-willed (I am god) spirit of rebelliousness. But, not all preachers have thrown in the towel. Some have come out of the closet—on fire—dedicated to cleanse the house of God.

As the end approaches, the gap is widening between those in sheep's clothing and the true servants of God. The gap is pretty wide at the present, but as it continues to widen, two very distinct camps will develop. It will become very unpopular to be numbered with the camp of true Bible believers. For example, we all have witnessed the division that "Christian Rock" has created.

The attack upon the believers has already started, but will intensify until the followers of Jesus will become the world's most hated and despised people. Jesus warned us that such a day would come for the Church. "Then shall they deliver you up to be afflicted, and shall kill you: and ye shall be hated of all nations for my name's sake" (Matt. 24:9).

Hatred will fully manifest against God's people as the "community" of "the world's church" is set up. God's people are going to be lied about, framed, slan-

dered, humiliated and made a spectacle of before the
world in every crucifying way possible. Satan will turn
the heat of persecution up on God's people as far as
he has power to take it. Satan's end-time plan is to
destroy the world and its inhabitants, including the
"faithful" ones.

He wishes only to thwart the purpose of God, thus
preventing the Second Coming of Jesus. If the Church
fails to achieve the spiritual victory designed of God,
then Jesus cannot come, the dead cannot be made
perfect (to receive their resurrected bodies), and Satan
will become the complete master of the earth. The
saints who will overcome this hour of great temptation
must flee to Jesus and seek the shelter of His blood,
and come out of Babylon to find their place of refuge
in His everlasting arms.

Many Christians and their church organizations have
made a great sacrifice. They have built schools and
taken on the burden of educating their own children
as they witnessed the educational system in America
become rotten to the core with humanism and New
Age propaganda. The brainwashing of the American
youth is an ongoing sinister plot to prepare them for
the "New World" and make them willing subjects and
participants in its paganistic lifestyle.

The battle for the minds of the youth began over
a generation ago, when the NEA (National Education
Association) adopted as their philosophic platform, John
Dewey's concepts of humanism, socialism, and a one
world order. Every book sanctioned by the NEA, for
the past half century, has been dedicated to the undermining of the liberties of the nation, the students,
personal patriotism, and their faith in God. John Dewey,
while working on the philosophy of education for
America, was at the same time going to Russia and
assisting in the development and organization of the
Marxist educational system.

Billions and billions of dollars have been spent by these "anti-Christ Americans," such as the Rockefellers, to alter the conscience of Americans and to slowly undermine the biblical heritage of our nation. Today, they are well on their way to having accomplished their objectives of enslaving the minds and "the thinking" of the average American citizen. Daniel said that the beast would "wear out the saints" of God. The "battle" for the minds of Americans is through television, music, printed media, institutions of learning, drugs and alcohol. What the government has done, along with liberal Christians, is to prepare millions of innocent Americans to blindly and wilfully embrace the coming snare of the "mark of the beast."

The controlling and influencing grip of the seven heads which John saw on the beast has, with money and influence, strangled the institutions of the land and in almost every strategic position they have placed one of their own. The doctrines of the anti-Christ have filled the airways, the printed page in America, and most parts of the world, as he prepares the hearts of men to receive his coming kingdom.

These seven heads of the beast which John saw were the mountains of world-dominating power which would ensnare the world. Even the coming world religion will be wined, financed, and supported by these heads. The control of these seven heads is very near a perfect consolidation. The beast has its people in place. Many Christians have lost their will to resist. The influence of the seven heads has gradually recreated a new mindset in the American people, where the Bible message has been intentionally ignored, ridiculed, and despised.

Americans have been taught to put their trust in what they know and in people or the government who have instructed them these many years. In this we see a substitution of one's faith having been cunningly achieved. Our dollar bills may yet, for the time being, still read "In God We Trust," but for most Americans it has come to read, "In Myself and My Government I Trust and Depend."

Look in comparison to the spirit that has overtaken our nations and the minds and hearts of many Christians with the spirit of the Apostle Paul. "But we had the sentence of death in ourselves, that we should not trust in ourselves, but in God which raiseth the dead" (2 Cor. 1:9). "Not that we are sufficient of ourselves to think anything as of ourselves; but our sufficiency is of God" (2 Cor. 3:5).

Paul warned us that our faith must not stand in the wisdom of men, but in the power of God. Yet, we have allowed the spirit of the world to so saturate our souls that we see or experience little or none of the power of God. Without which we most assuredly will fall into the snare of this final hour. The Apostle John has made it clear that it is only by our faith that we shall overcome the wicked world about us. "Who is he that overcometh the world: and this is the victory that overcometh the world, even our faith" (1 John 5:4).

The end-time entrapment, prepared by the devil, has been laid through the society about us. His plan has been to blend our lives into the society, until we think, act, and behave as does the world about us. The power and influence of our present environment is touching every emotion of the natural man. Few realize just how much the society has drugged their mind and spirit. Satan's influence has been so overpowering that the vast majority cannot get enough of the world and the manner of life it is offering.

This, in turn, has for the past generation or so, developed the most selfish, prideful, impatient, spoiled, disrespectful, and ungodly (by biblical standards) people that this nation has ever seen. We have become a nation of pleasure lovers, more than lovers of God. Except we repent and abandon our worshiping the ways of the world, we shall not be able to overcome this final hour of temptation which has come upon us. We need to meditate one more time on the warning Jesus gave. He knew we would be the people to whom His words would apply.

> Heaven and earth shall pass away: but my words shall not pass away.

> And take heed to yourselves, lest at any time your hearts be overcharged with surfeiting, and drunkenness, and cares of this life, and so that day come upon you unawares.

> For as a snare shall it come on all them that dwell on the face of the whole earth.

> Watch ye therefore, and pray always, that ye may be accounted worthy to escape all these things that shall come to pass, and to stand before the Son of man. (Luke 21:33-36)

Chapter Six

The Beast that
Rose Up Out of the Sea

The "mark of the beast" does not make much sense until we have a working conception of who the beast actually is. Then, we can observe his movements and warn our neighbor of the deceiving process by which he plans to ensnare the world. The finding of the beast can only begin in the Bible, because it is the Bible which has revealed that the beast would come. But, in our study of the Bible, we must remain dependent upon the prophetic information the Bible provides. We must also thoroughly evaluate the details of that prophetic information within the framework of history to which the prophecy is directed. Then, our interpretations will have to check and balance with the details the prophets have given.

When we become careless and overassumptive, and begin to ignore even one detail thinking it may not be significant, then we will in some measure go astray in our interpretations. One of the great dangers in the study of prophecy is to start not from the Bible, but, from some long-standing popular interpretation.

The Bible tells us that there have been four great world beastly powers which preceded and prepared the way for the last great beastly kingdom (Dan. 7). The Lord gave the prophet Daniel a vision of the beasts; who they were and the order in which they would come.

> Daniel spake and said, I saw in my vision by
> night, and, behold, the four winds of the heaven
> strove upon the great sea. And four great beasts
> came out of the sea, diverse one from another.
> The first was like a lion, and had eagles wings.
> (Dan. 7:2-4)

This first beast was Babylon.

> And behold another beast, a second, like to a
> bear. (Dan. 7:5)

This second beast was Persia.

> After this I beheld, and lo another, like a leop-
> ard, which had upon the back of it four wings
> of a fowl; the beast had also four heads; and
> dominion was given to it. (Dan. 7:6)

This third beast was Greece, primarily, Alexander
the Great. Later his kingdom would be divided amongst
his four great generals, represented by the four heads.

> And after this I saw in the night visions, and
> behold a fourth beast, dreadful and terrible,
> and strong exceedingly; and it had great iron
> teeth: . . . It was diverse from all the beasts that
> were before it; and it had ten horns. (Dan. 7:7)

This fourth beast was the Roman Empire.

Now, Daniel describes the rising of a great end-
time beast. Before we continue with Daniel, it is interesting to note that as the Apostle John described this
end-time beast, he reveals its awesomeness by combin-
ing all the former world kingdoms into one, by birthing,
him from the fourth (Rome), and then as a leopard
(Greece), a bear (Persia), and finally, as a lion (Babylon)
(Rev. 13:2).

This beast or horn would arise out of the ten toes
(kings) of the fourth. The toes were a mixture of iron
and clay. Such elements will not adhere very well. These
ten toes which Daniel saw would in time become the

ten little kingdoms from which this powerful beast would arise. These kingdoms in time emerged out of the old Roman Empire.

Now, back to Daniel: "I considered the horns, and, behold, there came up among them another 'little horn,' before whom there were three of the first horns plucked up by the roots: and, behold, in this horn were eyes like the eyes of a man, and a mouth speaking great things" (Dan. 7:8). Daniel saw to the end of time and the burning of the beast, the same thing which John saw in Revelation 19:20.

Daniel was desirous to know the truth of the ten horns and of the "little horn" which came up out of them and before whom three of the ten horns fell. Daniel says that he wants to know about that horn that had eyes, and a mouth that spake very great things, whose look was more stout than his fellows. Then Daniel says that "the ten horns out of this kingdom (Rome) are ten kings that shall arise: and another shall rise after them; and he shall be diverse from the first, and he shall subdue three kings" (Dan. 7:24).

Daniel in verse 11 had called this horn a beast (meaning a violent rain or storm), the other four beasts were great earthly kingdoms, and this horn would in the eyes of Daniel, become a kingdom far stronger than the ten from which he would rise. He would be a great earthly kingdom, which in his rising appeared to be very harmless; Daniel at first described him as a little horn with a big mouth. This country of America certainly has a big mouth today. If you don't believe me, just ask the rest of the world. They will be very obliging, and perhaps shocking in what they would have to say about this little horn. When America speaks, the rest of the world listens. They might not agree, but they listen.

The prophet Daniel, also, saw that the horn had the eyes of a man. No nation has ever covered the

whole world with the thoroughness of surveillance as
has the United States. Today, we watch the world, from
the sky, from the ground and from under the sea, the
world over. But, America has even spied out its own
people. Today, there is no more individual privacy; the
government has details of information on every individual. The eyes of the beast are most definitely running to and fro throughout the earth.

Let us return to Daniel as he further identifies this
horn. This horn shall rise after the ten, as well as out
from them. The ten were part of the original Roman
Empire. Europe and Eastern Europe primarily were
made of these ten kingdoms. Therefore, this horn would
arise out of these ten horns. All ten of them would in
some way contribute to the rise of this great beast. We
understand this because Daniel is very clearly revealing
that he would come up out of these ten horns. Daniel
distinctly tells us that this "horn" is not a confederation
of the ten kingdoms, but a separate nation or kingdom
altogether.

This is further born out when Daniel reveals that
this horn shall subdue three of the ten kings or three
of the other horns (Dan. 7:24). We already know that
this horn is an earthly kingdom, which arose very inno-
cently, and now had risen to such a stature that it had
developed the capability to overcome three of the original ten nations from which it had been birthed.

If the reader has studied American history he will
know that the only great world power which has arisen
out of Europe and in turn had to defeat three of those
kings to emerge upward into its great throne in the
world, has been no other nation, than the United States
of America. And, as you know, in the rising to nation-
hood, America is the only great power that defeated
three of the ten horns of the old Roman Empire. The
United States defeated England, France, and Spain and
subdued them upon her own soil. The United States

primarily defeated Germany, Italy, and Japan in World War II. But, all three of those nations were not the toes of the Roman beast.

Just because America has become the great end-time beast who continues to manipulate the world by her great mouth, her money and her sword does not mean that God has not used this country for special purposes of His own. It is clear in Scripture that He used Babylon and Persia to accomplish things for Him. Nor can we deny that great missionary efforts have gone forth from her shores. But, that witness has not been going forth from the United States embassies, etc.

Today, like no other day in our history, one can see that the sins of America have reached unto heaven, and her abominations have spread throughout the earth. This nation has risen up to play. She is drunk on the wine of her own fornication and slowly, but surely, Satan has prepared her as the instrument through which he is deceiving the whole earth. He is using her wealth and influence to lay his final "snare."

Satan has been carefully executing his plan through this beast, the "leader of the world," by the means of her power and her glory (influence) to unite the nations into a one world system. This rising system is already overspreading and implementing controls that will very soon affect every major part of man's life upon the whole earth. John saw this when the beast with its seven heads of power would supervise the rising of a second beast. This second beast will be given all the power of the first beast (Rev. 13:12).

The Apostle John's writing of this end-time super-power declared, "And I stood upon the sand of the sea, and saw a beast rise up out of the sea, having seven heads and ten horns, and upon his horns ten crowns, and upon his heads the name of blasphemy. And the beast which I saw was like unto a leopard, and

his feet were as the feet of a bear, and his mouth as the
mouth of a lion: and the dragon gave him his power,
and his seat, and great authority" (Rev. 13:1-2).

The Seven Heads of Power

First Head—White House—State Department, Em-
bassies.
Second Head—Federal Reserve System—(Interna-
tional Banks).
Third Head—CIA, FBI, etc.
Fourth Head—Military, Pentagon.
Fifth Head—Major Corporations, etc.
Sixth Head—Mass Communications, etc.
Seventh Head—Council on Foreign Relations, Tri-
lateral Commission.

The above have for the past generation politically
and militarily manipulated and controlled the earth.
The ten horns which the beast has upon his head could
be the ten kingdoms from which she sprang (Europe),
or it could represent the ten regions which the world
has been secretly divided into for the New World Order.
Just how far these ten world regions or kingdoms have
moved toward realization only a select few truly know.
But, as we keep our eyes on certain parts of the world
which needs to be softened up or destabilized, there
you will see war and oppression develop. The author
is suspicious of any military conflict which breaks out
upon the earth. More than 50 percent of the time it is
part of the end-time plan and strategy of the beast's
operation to weaken certain nations for the coming
world order.

There are two ways the new one world system deals
with nations. One, by leading the nations of the earth
into horrendous levels of debt. Two, by disintegrating
what once were strong countries with terrorism, em-
bargoes, and war (James Perloff, *Shadows of Power*
[Appleton, WI: Western Islands]: 212). Last year alone

there were over seventy major military conflicts throughout the earth.

Region I—The United States of America
Region II—The United Nations of Europe
Region III—The United Kingdom of Japan
Region IV—The United Kingdom of South Africa,
    Australia and New Zealand
Region V—The United States of the Socialist Re-
    public
Region VI—The United States of South America
Region VII—The United Arab Kingdoms
Region VIII—The United Kingdom of Central Af-
    rica
Region IX—The United Kingdom of India and
    Southeast Asia
Region X—The United Kingdom of China

From the present structure of the United Nations
we understand that the most influential of the above
ten are, America, Russia, Europe, China, and Japan.
The above ten kingdoms may yet go through certain
alterations before their final consolidation as the New
World Order (Rev. 17:12). Even though the United
States is represented as one of the geographical regions or horns of the beast, it does not change the fact
that as Satan brings together the unification of his
world system, the United States will have been the
number one instrument in making it happen.

The truth of the matter is, there could not have
been a world government unless the United States had
led the way. In the final analysis, the beast's power and
image will be reflected in its worldwide administrative
organization. The evil self-seeking corrupted men who
have yielded themselves into the hands of the dragon,
to be his servants, will be as kings or presidents over
these regions. They will utilize threats of trade embar-
goes, military action, withholding loans, etc., in order
to bring the nations in line.

The present headquarters of the first beast which John saw is without question centered in the United States. The locating of the United Nations in New York City was carefully planned by the heads of the first beast. The United States' footing of most of the cost of the United Nations was, also, by design. But, the spirit of the United Nations is revealed in the people who founded this monster from hell. All were Internationalists, Communists or Communist sympathizers.

I do not see Europe as the center of the second beast, unless, for some reason Satan would choose to switch the location of his headquarters. If, for some reason New York City was burned or it had served its purpose, then we could see a transfer of the seat of Satan's authority: the financial control of the world could be switched from New York City to possibly Brussels. But, that would not at all imply that the European Common Market was the beast. The ECM is going to be only one of the ten regions.

United Nations

The main political and administrative organization that the beast (U.S.) is presently transferring its power to, is the United Nations. This organization was formed when Harry S. Truman (Mason and Globalist) signed the new United Nations Charter, on 14 December 1946, which had been written by Alger Hiss and Harry Dexter White, who soon after were convicted as Communist spies. The United Nations at that time accepted a gift of 8.6 million dollars from John D. Rockefeller, Jr., to purchase eighteen acres of land along the East River in New York City. The next year the U.S. Congress approved 65 million dollars of interest-free money which went to finance the construction of the United Nations headquarters building. So, we see from the Apostle John's revelation that another beast would arise: he would execute the authority of the first beast (Rev. 13).

The United States has been the number one financial supporter of the United Nations ever since. As a
matter of fact, had not the United States underwritten
its costs, the United Nations would have folded up a
long time ago. We need to ask ourselves why have the
leaders in America been willing to finance an institution whose constitution is diametrically opposed to its
own constitution?

As we watch the unfolding of world events today,
and the efforts of George Bush, Bill Clinton, and others to increase the political and military authority of
the United Nations, there is little room for doubt that
the United Nations which John witnessed arising out
of the earth was birthed in deception, from the minds
of evil and designing men. John wrote, "And I beheld
another beast coming up out of the earth; and he had
two horns like a lamb, and he spake as a dragon. And
he exerciseth all the power of the first beast before
him, and causeth the earth and them which dwell therein
to worship the first beast, whose deadly wound was
healed" (Rev. 13:11-12).

The word "worship" in Greek means to "kiss," or
"like a dog licking his master's hand." The United Nations has been a clever tool utilized by the unseen
rulers of the government of the United States to bring
the rest of the world in, "wine and dine them," and
cause their leaders to worship the beast. That is, to
want the affluent kind of society here in America, as
well as, protection from Russia! The deception has
worked almost to perfection, as these nations of the
earth have been willing to mortgage the souls of their
own people to have the lifestyle and enjoy the pleasure
of feasting with the beast.

The United Nations is only a breath away from
becoming a world government. She consists of 159
nations—nearly every country in the world. Its internal
organization focuses upon every facet of our personal

lives. What the United Nations lacks is the military muscle to make it a feared and respected power. President Clinton is presently doing all that he can to see that the United Nations is given that muscle. Clinton's strategy is to place the military forces of the United States under the control of the United Nations, and take the control away from the American people to whom it belongs. If he accomplishes this, then, America's own soldiers can be used against the American people when the United Nations would consider it expedient. We presently have a few congressmen and senators who see what is happening and are fighting to keep this traitorous act from being committed by the president. It is now so late and the night so far spent, that little can be done to prevent the sovereignty of the United States from being swallowed down the mouth of this second beast.

It is pretty well known that the United States has for several years been under the control of a very few select and extremely powerful men. These men, from behind the scenes, are controlling the major banking corporations of the world. The United States fell into their grasp when a pressured and a deceived Congress in 1913 passed the Federal Reserve Act. Charles Lindbergh would later state that this act established the most gigantic trust on earth and legalized the invisible government of the monetary power.

Woodrow Wilson

The twenty-eighth president of the United States, Woodrow Wilson, did not receive the majority of the popular vote but was put in by the electoral. Wilson was not as smart as Andrew Jackson, nor Abraham Lincoln and certainly did not have the patriotic commitment in his heart as did the former presidents. He was the one who sold this nation down the river to the super rich who own and control the Federal Reserve System.

Apparently, Wilson would later come to his senses, only then it was far too late. He would later acknowledge that, "We have come to be one of the worst ruled, one of the most completely controlled governments in the civilized world—no longer a government of free opinion, no longer a government by a vote of the majority, but a government by the opinion and duress of a small group of dominant men" (National Economy and the Banking system, Senate Documents, col. 3, no. 23 75th Congress, 1st Session, 1939).

But, Wilson was also deeply troubled about an influence that was even more pervasive. In his book, *The New Freedom*, he wrote,

> Some of the biggest men in the United Sates, in the field of commerce and manufacture are afraid of something. They know that there is a power so organized, so subtle, so watchful, so interlocked, so complete, so pervasive, that they had better not speak above their breath when they speak in condemnation of it. (Woodrow Wilson, *The New Freedom* [New York: Double Day, 1914], 13-14)

Woodrow Wilson was the culprit that turned this wild animal loose in America. I guess we should appreciate the fact that he later warned us that the "thing" is out there somewhere, just don't talk about it above a whisper.

This, dear reader, is exactly what the Apostle John saw. It doesn't matter how righteous a nation may begin, but what happens to it as time goes by.

In 1971, the *New York Times* magazine reported that Congressman Louis McFadden, chairman of the House Committee on Banking and Currency from 1920 to 1931 remarked that the passage of the Federal Reserve Act brought about a superstate controlled by international bankers and international industrialists, acting together to enslave the world for their own pleasure. In the 1960s, Congressman Wright Patman, former chairman of the House Banking Committee, and a powerful critic of the central banking system agreed.

> Today, in the United States, we have in effect two governments—we have the duly constituted government—then, we have an independent, uncontrolled and uncoordinated government in the federal reserve system operating the money powers which are reserved to congress by the Constitution. (William T. Still, *New World Order* [Lafayette, LA: Huntington House Publishers, 1990], 150)

Presently, the United States is in debt to these "satanic enterprising vultures" somewhere between five and six trillion dollars. If you could spend one million dollars a year it would take you one million years at that rate to spend a trillion dollars. This year alone the taxpayers of the United States will pay these owners of the Federal Reserve $400 *billion* in interest alone. Within only three years these leaches who now manage and control most of the world, including this great beast that John saw, will put into their coffers over a trillion dollars of the hard-earned money of the American people. The majority of this money will be used to further finance their coming world kingdom. They really do not care how many lives it may take or the sorrow they bring upon humanity.

These men buy and sell nations and presidents, including the United States. Not only is America and its people in financial slavery to them, but, so is most of the world. Their global one world government, which was preached so openly by George Bush, will in the very near future have attained the collective support necessary to take full control of the world. The machinery is in place, but, it will not happen until the appointed time on God's calendar has arrived. Evil of this magnitude does not go unchecked by God Himself.

There is presently a world parliament, fully organized to instantly step in and implement the New World
Order. But the whole process appears to be emerging
gradually due to the mindset of the people throughout
the world being developed into one of global con-
sciousness. The tragedy of this whole scenario is that
many of these globalists think the problems in the
world have reached such proportions that unless a world
government is set up to deal with the problems on an
international scale with international authority, the earth
as we know it is doomed to destruction and ruin. This
again is another means being used to justify controlling the earth.

What so many of these sincere people, who have
embraced this doctrine, do not understand is that these
wicked men, with wealth in high places, could easily
solve these problems if they had a mind to do so. But,
they do not, and are using this propaganda to leverage
the creation of a system which will give them power to
control and manipulate the earth. This organization
belongs to Satan and he is giving unto it tremendous
power so that his evil purposes will be realized. The
Bible tells us "the love of money is the root of all evil"
(1 Tim. 6:10). The international Masonic bankers have
such a passion for money, that they will commit any
atrocity necessary to get their hands on the wealth of
the nations.

The new coming world government has prepared
a number of fundamental articles by which they will
operate. A couple of these articles are given here for
the readers consideration. Keep in mind that these
have been constructed for the basic purpose of selling
the world government to the nations.

Article 1: As soon as ten national governments
have given provisional ratification to the constitution for the federation of earth, and have also
ratified world legislative bills #1, #6, #7, and

#11 (this act), then an earth financial credit corporation shall be organized and activated as a division of the world economic development organization, for the purpose of introducing the new earth finance, credit, money and banking system. (I personally believe the method of monetary exchange from top to bottom is already set. The way they plan to take the rest of the wealth of the American people has long ago left the drawing board.) . . .

Article 3: Initial revolving lines of credit in earth dollars shall be calculated on the basis of $1 billion dollars for each million of population for countries having natural population increase rates by birth of more than 2% annually, $1.5 billion dollars per million of population for countries having natural population increase rates between 1% and 2%, $2 billion dollars per million of population for countries having natural population increase rates of between 0% and 1%, and $2.5 billion dollars per million of population for countries having zero or less population growth. (Gary H. Kah, *En Route to Global Occupation* [Lafayette, LA: Huntington House Publishers, 1992], 203)

The above incentives would certainly motivate most nations to abort babies and take whatever measures might become necessary in order to qualify. Article 3 is a diabolic mark against the unborn, as well as, potential parents. Maybe this article would help a lot of Americans to understand why Bill and Hillary are so pro-abortion.

The Two Horns of the Second Beast

The Apostle John said that the second beast would have two horns like a lamb. Lambs are always such sweet innocent little creatures. How could a lamb be dangerous? This lamb which John saw had two horns. The foremost concern of the United Nations, the coming New World Order, is to finally have their horns in place. Horns symbolize national power. This second beast will have two nations which will become its means of power. The two horns that John saw would be these two great nations coming together to give the united strength necessary to control the world. When the plans of the United Nations were laid it was their main objective to utilize Russia as a tool to destabilize nations by war and make it appear that America would be the great saviour. What nations did America save since the rise of the United Nations? South Korea (discussed in the next chapter), barely, because the United Nations was calling all the shots. Now, that the world is sufficiently deceived and war torn, they are ready to come under a world government. What more glorious way could this possibly transpire than for Russia and the United States to become friends at last, when all along they were horns of the same beast. The United States was the positive influence—Russia was the negative—and together the world would be frightened and herded into one big camp. The white horse of Revelation has been trotting around for a long time deceiving the earth.

Franklin D. Roosevelt and all his roundtable friends had long conspired together. One only need read what Roosevelt and the rest of the internationalists have given Russia, to understand what was going on. The truth is told as one watched the most powerful nation on the face of the earth, turn its head time and time again since 1945 as Russia overthrew nation after nation while the international bankers were footing the bill with the money from the United States taxpayers. The sickening fact is that every president of the United States, did in some way assist the atrocities which Russia has committed throughout the earth. Most of the presidents did not just stand by with folded hands, but dipped their hands into the blood of those nations and are continuing to do so today. It is unbelievable how so many who call themselves Americans have sold their souls to the devil.

The United Nations, as John saw, came upon the earth like a lamb. But eventually John says that the lamblike organization would speak as a dragon; that powerful creature is just about to open its mouth. The world for the first time will witness its awesome teeth. Because, as John prophesied the first beast (the United States) would give to the second beast (the United Nations) all of its power (Rev. 13:12). I believe this will happen sometime between now and Passover of the year A.D. 2000.

A Speaking Image

John saw that an "image" would be invented, which would in his mind become a unique instrument of power in the hands of the beast. To John this image or invention appeared to live. What better way to describe the electronic age and its awesome demonstration of power, than an image which did both live and speak. An image with the means of its electrical ability could cause the whole world to become individually controlled, to such an extreme, that no one would be able to buy or sell without a number which communicated with this image or licked its hand like a dog.

There is little question that John was seeing the computer age and the sophistication of our modern age of technology. He was seeing how Satan would maneuver his end-time instruments, the United States and the United Nations, to enslave the world. This enslaving process would have the appearance of being as harmless as a lamb. This little lamblike strategy, together with the technological know-how, will enable the second beast to captivate the world.

In verse 5 of the thirteenth chapter of Revelation, John makes a very provocative statement: that after a period of perhaps years of development and preparation of the first beast by Satan, the time would come when Satan would give to the first beast all his power for forty-two months. This is understood as a literal period of three-and-a-half years.

The First Beast

But, before the period of forty-two months arrives and Satan bestows his full power upon the beast, John gives revealing information about the first beast. John said that he saw one of his heads, as it were, wounded to death; and his deadly wound was healed. Shortly after the healing all the world wondered after the beast. In Revelation 13:14, John said that it was a wound created by a sword. This tells us that it was a military wound, no doubt, received through war or an attack. But, the wound created by the sword was quickly healed.

On 7 December 1941, the United States experienced a devastating wound to its military head. The military strength of the United States was so weakened by this attack, that had the Japanese fully comprehended what they had accomplished, they could have easily taken Pearl Harbor and launched an invasion on the West Coast. But, in a matter of weeks the United States recovered. Not only did she recover, but, won two wars on two fronts simultaneously and stunned the world with the dropping of two atomic bombs on Japan.

Then John says, "All the world wondered after the beast. . . . And they worshipped the beast, saying, who is like unto the beast? Who is able to make war with him?" (Rev. 13:3, 4). Some have said, but, what about Russia. Well, if Mexico had been given what Roosevelt gave to Russia, Mexico would have had the atomic bomb and military machine just like Russia came to have (William T. Still, *New World Order*, p. 163-174).

Americans just have not known what has and is going
on.

The whole story about Pearl Harbor, for example,
has never been told to the American people. Most
believed what we had been told by the news media. For
several weeks prior to 7 December 1941, Roosevelt
and the Secretary of War, Henry L. Stimson, and others had tried to determine a way to get the Japanese to
attack us. The problem in the United States was that
over 80 percent of the American people did not want
the United States to get involved in the war in Europe.
Since Italy, Japan and Germany had signed a treaty to
defend each other, one way to bring the United States
into the war in Europe was to maneuver Japan into
attacking the United States. Stimson wrote in his diary
on 25 November 1941, nearly two weeks before Pearl
Harbor was bombed, the following: "The question was
how we should maneuver them into a position of firing
the first shot without allowing too much danger to
ourselves. It was a difficult proposition." The United
States had cracked the Japanese code more than a year
before and knew the attack was coming. The information of the attack was kept from the high command in
Pearl Harbor. That is one reason so many of our ves-
sels were totally unprepared when the attack occurred.
The death of the American soldiers can be laid at the
feet of Roosevelt and the godless Council on Foreign
Relations.

Since World War II, the United States has been the
leader of the world and has spread its political power
and degrading lifestyle throughout the earth. The world
has lusted after her riches, her ways, and her glory.
Although the United States (the first beast) would be
able to have a great effect upon the world, she would
need the instrumentality of the second beast and the
unique "image" (computer), to be able to subdue the
earth. There is no doubt that the computer has the

means to cause all, both small and great, rich and poor, free and bond, to receive a "mark" in their right hand or in their foreheads. The dependency upon this device is growing at an alarming rate. Preparations are well advanced to utilize this electronic means to manipulate the masses for political, economic, and religious ends.

The Marking

The computer or the "image" as John saw will exercise all the authority (in all seven heads, in milliseconds of time) for the first beast (Rev. 13:12). Now, the power of the first beast will exercise his dominion with such skill and precision that the apostle must have stood aghast at what he saw. Not only did he witness the control of the entire world under the minute supervision of this great system, he also beheld a monitoring of all individuals. A monitoring so minute and accurate, that no one could participate in society without legal authority and proper identification from the electronic "image" of this world system.

The apostle foretold that the beastly system would cause all, both small and great, rich and poor, free and bond (Rev. 13:17), to bow down and submit to his way of life. Soon everything in the entire United States and the world will be marked and controlled by this system of power.

When Satan has accomplished his goal of computerization of the whole world, then the snare will have been laid. Everything bought and sold will have to be scanned as it is presently being done in many stores all across this country (Rev. 13:14–18).

> The path to 100 percent electronic money, and total government financial control of citizens, as Harvey Wachsman explained in the *New York Times* article, is Americard—a "smart card" that does it all. Cash is freedom! A man without

money is free to do very little. If modern electronic credit and debit cards can be substituted
for cash, then every financial transaction of your
life can be catalogued and stored for future
reference and those with the power to cut off
your access to electronic money can strangle
you in a heartbeat. The potential for totalitarian blackmail and control is incredible—but most
Americans don't even seem to notice. (Donald
S. McAlvany, *Toward A New World Order* [Phoe-
nix, AZ: Western Pacific], 68)

The "mark" will be presented as a complete necessity for saving the government billions of dollars, and
expediting all the transactions of society. The coordi-
nation of it all will bring a more functional and practical world. The "smart card" will probably come first
and shortly thereafter will come the implantation of
some laser mark. The card may not prove real practical
as it can be stolen and may be duplicated. It may have
to be rapidly abandoned for the mark. The mark will,
no doubt, initiate the beginning of the beast's forty-two
months of world domination, which will only be possible by the entrapment of all the nations of the earth
into a well-schemed plan of centralized control by these
"lovers of money and power" (Rev. 13:11).

If everything is moving in agreement with the chronology as presented in chapter 2, the mark will become
law some time around the year 2000. But, if not, it will
come shortly thereafter. This attack by Satan with the
mark will be his most deceptive and forceful effort to
ensnare the people of God.

A World Religion

The merging of the religions of the world has been
one of the major concerns of the United Nations since
their inception. They have had a religious affairs department, focusing upon the unification of all religions,

feverishly at work for nearly a half century. They are well down the road to accomplishing their objective.

We read of a great deal of dialogue going on between pagans and Christians throughout the world, and even of common or community worshipping. Each, of course, in one common meeting worships his own particular god. True Christians full of the Holy Ghost know that there is no fellowship between light and darkness. Gradually we are witnessing the coming of that woman John saw. "I will shew unto thee the judgment of the great whore that sitteth upon many waters: (people) . . . and I saw a woman sit upon a scarlet colored beast, . . . and the woman was arrayed in purple and scarlet color, and decked with gold and precious stones and pearls, having a golden cup in her hand full of abominations and filthiness of her fornication" (Rev. 17:1, 3–4). But, the fact that John saw the woman (end-time apostate religion) riding upon the back of the beast insinuates that religion will be a high riding part of the New World Order.

What liberal and worldly Christians fail to grasp is that to snub and ignore the centrality of the Blood of Jesus will cause them to fulfill the above. John saw a close relationship develop between the beast and Satan's bride. This false church would be found preaching a gospel which would agree with the spirit of the beast.

When the seven heads of the beast have become solidified so that each head and horn has been bonded together and given over to the control of the second beast, then the plans of Satan can take full advantage of the electronic system. When the "mark of the beast" is ready to be implemented, there will come with it the religious seal and power of Satan. Most Christians know what happened to Judas at the Passover with Jesus and the disciples. It was there that he stepped a little too far to the "left" and the Bible says that Satan entered into him. I believe that is what will happen to every person who receives the mark. Perhaps at first the demonic possession will not be noticeable, but before long each individual will come to the realization that they have submitted themselves into the hands of a power from which they cannot free themselves.

The mark will have every appearance of being a natural and necessary thing to do. This governmental necessity will leave one with no other alternative, either to reject it, which will in time carry stiff and severe penalties, or submit to it.

John wrote that whoever would not "lick the hand of the beast like a dog" (worship) would be killed. I have found very few Christians who have given much thought to laying down their lives for what they believe.

Prophet Isaiah

The prophet Isaiah foresaw the day when the "mark of the beast" would come. God had revealed it as a covenant with death.

> Because ye have said, we have made a covenant with death, and with hell are we at agreement; when the overflowing scourge shall pass through, it shall not come unto us: for we have made lies our refuge, and under falsehood have we hid ourselves:
>
> Judgment also will I lay to the line, and righteousness to the plummet: and the hail shall sweep away the refuge of lies, and the waters shall overflow the hiding place.
>
> And your covenant with death shall be disanulled, and your agreement with hell shall not stand; when the overflowing scourge shall pass through, then ye shall be trodden down by it. (Isa. 28:15, 17-18)

I believe when this "covenant of death" is entered into with the beast, Satan will impart certain controlling spirits to indwell every person receiving the mark (Rev. 18:2). Satan will have marked his own. Everyone who has received the mark will begin to partake of his nature and evil will fill the Earth without measure. John described it thus, "Babylon the great is fallen, is fallen, and is become the habitation of devils, and the hold of every foul spirit" (Rev. 18:2).

To manage a corrupt world will always require measures to be taken, which will institute controls and disciplines which are believed by many to be necessary. But, in the spirit we can see a far more sinister power at work. This is what John saw, as well as, what many praying Christians are seeing today.

Six Six Six
6 6 6

Approximately nineteen hundred years ago the Apostle John, by the revelation of the Spirit of God, revealed the following: "Here is wisdom. Let him that hath understanding count the number of the beast: for it is the number of a man; and his number is six hundred threescore and six" (Rev. 13:18).

> Every universal product code has three uniden-tified marks whose number equivalent is "6" encoding it with the code number "6 6 6." The reason that computers work on a series of 6 cores like the supermarket model 304 produced by National Cash Register. It allows changing direction of current to performing switching operations. The 6 cores work in conjunction with 60 displacements x 6—one character—one bit of information. The formula for this system is 6, 60, 6. To number a card, person or item, the transaction must be prefixed "six hundred, threescore and six." That is an amazing correla-tion with what John saw and wrote concerning the electronic image that will someday be used

to control buying and selling. (Bob Fraley, *The Last Days in America* [Phoenix, AZ: Christian Life Service], 228)

The Eight Beasts

There will have been eight beast-nation powers which have ruled the Earth, since the beginning of Israel's birth into a nation (2000 B.C.), and their reign will continue unto the end of the Gentile world as we know it. The apostle spoke of these nations in the Book of Revelation:

> And there are seven kings: five are fallen, and one is, and the other is not yet come; and when he cometh, he must continue a short space.
>
> And the beast that was, and is not, even he is the eighth, and is of the seven, and goeth into perdition.
>
> And the ten horns which thou sawest are ten kings, which have received no kingdom as yet; but receive power as kings one hour with the beast.
>
> These have one mind, and shall give their power and strength unto the beast. (Rev. 17:10–13)

The Eight Kingdoms

The first kingdom-beast was Egypt
The second kingdom-beast was Assyria
The third kingdom-beast was Babylon
The fourth kingdom-beast was Persia
The fifth kingdom-beast was Greece
The sixth kingdom-beast was Rome
The seventh kingdom-beast is America
The eighth kingdom-beast is the United Nations

The Apostle John said in Revelation 17:10, that five of the kings had fallen. That is to say, that in John's day, Egypt, Assyria, Babylon, Persia, and Greece had come and gone. John was living in the midst of the sixth beast, Rome, so he says, "and one is."

The next thing which John wrote was, "the other (the seventh) is not yet come; and when he cometh, he must continue a short space." When we consider how long some of the other empires or kingdoms lasted, then two hundred to three hundred years is not very long. If the United States gives her sovereignty to the United Nations in the year 2000, then our nation will have lived for 224 years.

In verse 11, John wrote that the beast that is not, even he is the eighth. We read elsewhere in the Book of Revelation that John likens this great end-time nation unto Babylon the great.

In Daniel we read that the first Babylon was symbolized as the head of pure gold. Both the head and the gold is very representative of the United States in her leadership and her wealth. John says the eighth beast is of the seven, and certainly of the seventh. It is true the United Nations has and will draw her vast means of wealth and power from those nations which once were part of the other seven.

There could not be a better description of the United Nations than she was of the seven. This eighth beast was created by the rich Socialists of America and Europe. She was birthed here in the land of the seventh and she continues to receive her life's blood from the wealth of this nation. The Americans who designed her continue to reign high above the pawns who carry out the political edicts. The eighth is of the seven. How true it is, and when the ten regions of the world are completely established and empowered, they shall reign one hour with the beast. This word "hour," means an instant or a short season. John had previously revealed that length of time to be three-and-a-half years, as did Daniel. We read both in Revelation, chapters eleven and thirteen, that the reign of the United Nations as a beast of world power will last three-and-a-half years.

If one prophetic hour equals three-and-a-half years and the seventh beast, the United States, gives up her sovereignty after 224 years, she will have lived for 64 prophetic hours.

This eighth beast John speaks of in the seventeenth chapter of Revelation, is the same beast that he was warning us of in the thirteenth chapter. The second beast in Revelation 13:11 is the same as the eighth beast of Revelation 17. This beast was to rise out of the earth. This word "earth" is, also, interpreted "country." The second beast has indeed risen out of the "country" of the first beast. We shall soon witness not only the transfer of power from the United States (the first and seventh beast), but also from all the remaining nations which today occupy the same geographical territory of the other six into the hands of the final eighth beast. This eighth beast is the United Nations, which the Apostle John saw rising up out of the earth (Rev. 13), which will cause all to receive the electronic mark in order to buy and sell.

Chapter Seven

The Rising of the Second Beast

The world has been warned for over nineteen hundred years that a political system would arise upon the earth wielding power so great, that all the earth would become its captive. The mighty roar of this dragon, even now, is being felt and heard throughout the world. The Apostle John saw the rising of this satanic monster: "And I beheld another beast coming up out of the earth; and he had two horns like a lamb, and he spake as a dragon" (Rev. 13:11).

If the American people had known the intentions of the planners of the United Nations, as well as, the diabolical goal of this fiendish organization, they would have risen up in great wrath and cast it into the sea. But since the United Nations was born in deception and intentionally founded upon our soil by the first beast, most Americans trusted that we would some how keep this "lamb" that John saw fenced inside Manhattan Island.

But, what we did not know was that this institution was fundamentally spawned by Americans whose patriotism was political, and who were so intoxicated by their wealth and lust for power, that their sole desire was to rule and control the earth. These men were, and are, so corrupt that the bed in which they sleep is covered with lies and deception.

When a patriotic American comes to understand that the United Nations has been designed to replace

the Constitution and Bill of Rights, with a totally different constitution and set of laws and completely destroy
the sovereignty of America, then they are beginning to
awaken to the horrendous deception which has been
imposed upon them by their trusted government.

The white horse and rider of deception has been
racing across our land and throughout the world for
the past eighty-five years. He made his first appearance
on the lawn of the White House in 1912. The rider was
none other than a Colonel House, who sold Woodrow
Wilson on giving control of the money of the American people to the international bankers. Thus, the
Federal Reserve System was born. Here is what Colonel House, the closest advisor to President Wilson
thought of the United States in 1913.

> America is the most undemocratic of democratic
> countries. . . . Our constitution and our laws
> served us well for the first hundred years of our
> existence, but under the conditions of today
> they are not only obsolete, but even grotesque.

He continues,

> nowhere in the world is wealth more defiant,
> and monopoly more insistent than in this mighty
> republic . . . and it is here that the next great
> battle for human emancipation will be fought
> and won. (Colonel Edward House, "Phillip Drug
> Administration," *A Story of Tomorrow* [New York,
> 1912], 222, 8)

There is absolutely no question that Colonel House
was at that moment in time the international bankers
undercover man. According to Prof. Charles Seymour,
House was the "unseen guardian angel" of the Federal
Reserve Act for the international bankers (the
Rockefellers, Kahns, Schiffs, Warburgs, and Morgans).

Colonel House was not only instrumental in the
formation of one of the heads of the first beast John

saw, but we learn that in the year 1921, Colonel House wrote the charter for the American branch of the "Round Table." This high-powered organization would later be incorporated as the Council on Foreign Relations (CFR). The CFR would also become one of the controlling heads of power of the first beast.

The awesomely powerful Council on Foreign Relations became the political invasion force for the Socialist elite international bankers in the United States. They had only five years previously financed and laid out the strategy for the overthrow of Russia and brought into being the second of the two horns John saw upon the head of the second beast. One year after the CFR was created they proclaimed the following:

> Obviously there is going to be no peace or prosperity for mankind as long as America remains divided into fifty or sixty independent states . . . equally obvious there is going to be no steady progress in civilization . . . until some kind of international system is created which will put an end to the diplomatic struggles incident to the attempt of every nation to make itself secure . . . the real problem today is that of world government. (Phillip Kerr, "From Empire to Commonwealth" [December 1922]: 97-98)

The white horse of the sixth seal of Revelation who had been prancing between Paris and New York City, is now into a "fox trot" headed toward the White House; the year is 1932. The new rider who climbs astride with the bow (snare) in his hand is Franklin D. Roosevelt.

The international bankers had chosen their man with care, but knew that unless some drastic changes were made in the minds of the American people, Roosevelt did not have a snail's chance of being elected. To effect the change, the "Socialist big boys" created a financial fiasco. They engineered the Crash of '29. Louis

McFadden, chairman of the House Banking Committee knew exactly who the culprits were. "It was not accidental. It was a carefully contrived occurrence . . . the international bankers sought to bring about a condition of despair here so that they might emerge as rulers of us all" (James Perloff, *The Shadows of Power: The Council on Foreign Relations and the American Decline* [Appleton, WI: Western Islands, 1988], 56).

The liberal press put the blame on the Republican administration and President Hoover. Hoover was a very well informed man. He was a true believer in the America of 1776, but he stood in the way of the world Socializers. Hoover had to be politically executed. His execution once again opened the gate to the "green pasture" in Washington, D.C., where this time far greater liberty and power would be given the horse and its new rider to roam, spreading its vial of deception.

The god of this world laid out his sinister plans to bring about World War II and those he used to finance the diabolical scheme were deep into the next phase even before the war was over. This next phase of deception would give rise to the second beast which John saw coming up out of the earth as a lamb with two horns. As vital and important a figure President Roosevelt was in the rise of the second beast, he was merely carrying out the orders which were being handed to him by his mentors, the CFR superelite.

In 1988 James Perloff wrote *The Shadows of Power: The Council on Foreign Relations and the American Decline*, revealing some of the key people behind the formation of the United Nations.

> In January 1943, Secretary of State Cordell Hull formed a steering committee composed of himself, Leo Pasvolsky, Isaiah Bowman, Sumner Welles, Norman Davis, and Morton Taylor. All of these men—with the exception of Hull—were

in the CFR. Later known as the informal agenda group, they drafted the original proposal for the United Nations. It was Bowman—a founder of the CFR and member of Colonel House's old "inquiry"—who first put forward the concept. They called in three attorneys, all CFR men, who ruled that it was constitutional. They discussed it with FDR on June 14, 1944. The president approved the plan, and announced it to the public that same day. (Ibid., 71)

The list of the United States delegates who participated in the formation of the United Nations were either members of the Council on Foreign Relations or later would be.

Theodore C. Achilles
James W. Angell
Hamilton Fish Armstrong
Charles E. Bohlen
Isaiah Bowman
Ralph Bunche
John M. Cabot
Mitchell B. Carroll
Andrew W. Cordier
John S. Dickey
John Foster Dulles
James Clement Dunn
Clyde M. Eichelberger
Muir S. Fairchild
Thomas K. Finletter
Artemus Gates
Arthur J. Hepburn
Julius C. Holmes
Philip C. Jessup
Joseph E. Johnson
R. Keith Kane
Foy D. Kohler
John E. Lockwood
Archibald Macleish
John J. McCloy
Cord Meyer, Jr.
Edward G. Miller, Jr.
Hugh Moore
Leo Pasvolsky
Dewitt C. Poole
William L. Ransom
Nelson A. Rockefeller
James T. Shotwell
Edward R. Stettinius, Jr.
Adlai E. Stevenson
Arthur Sweetser
James Swihart
Llewellyn E. Thompson
Herman B. Wells
Francis Wilcox
Charles W. Yost

(Lee, *United Nations Conspiracy* [Appleton, WI: Western Islands, 1981], 243)

The facts are that the formation of the United Nations was formed by a special group of men who danced to the same tune. The historical record clearly shows that the United Nations was a "demoniacal lamb" birthed first in the womb of the CFR for the purpose of establishing a totalitarian form of government through which Satan's chosen few could enslave the nations of the earth.

The war had been planned by the few, and had accomplished their evil desires. The war was over; the world had been conditioned. The time had come for the unveiling of the "lamb" of peace. Who would dare stand in the way of such a noble cause when so many millions lay dead throughout the earth. What a moment to deceive the earth.

But, there were very few Paul Reveres who had the horses available to them to go across the land to send out the alarm. But what warning was given so few listened; they were tired of war. They wanted a "saviour." They were ready to listen to the gospel that sounded from the mouth of this "saviour lamb" and the peace that he promised to bring.

It was on 25 April 1945, when the foul breath of the wolf in sheep's clothing, just as John foretold, began to fill the air. The rising of the second beast began just twelve days before Germany surrendered and only thirteen days after the death of Franklin Roosevelt. By 26 June this beast was taking his first steps, thanks to a nondiscerning and fool-hearted Congress and a president from Independence, Missouri, who had just recently been weaned from the fermented milk of Franklin Roosevelt.

The major sellout of the sovereignty of the United States began under the administrations of Franklin D. Roosevelt and Harry S. Truman, and has continued unchecked since that time. Today, Bill Clinton is trying to fulfill the dream of the past anti-Christ presidents of the United States. He plans to give full power and control of our military and government over into the hands of this monster that the apostle John saw rise up out of the sea (among people). A monster which would in time enslave the whole earth.

> In 1950 the state department issued a volume entitled Post-war Foreign Policy Preparation, 193945. It described in detail the policies and documents leading up to the creation of the United Nations and names the men who shaped these policies. This and similar official records reveal that the following men were key government figures in the United Nations planning within the United States state department and treasury department:

> Alger Hiss
> Virginius Frank Coe
> Noel Field
> Henry Julian Wadleigh
> John Carter Vincent
> William H. Taylor
> Harold Glasser
> Solomon Adler
> Abraham George Silverman
> Nathan Gregory Silvermaster
>
> Harry Dexter White
> Dean Acheson
> Laurence Duggan
> Victor Perlo
> David Weintraub
> Irving Kaplan
> William L. Ullman

> With the single exception of Dean Acheson, all of these men have since been identified in sworn testimony as secret communist agents! (G. Edward Griffin, *The Fearful Master* [Belmont, MA: Western Islands], 87)

But, when former Assistant Secretary of State Adolph Berle, Jr., testified before the House Committee on un-American activities, he described Dean Acheson as being responsible in heading up a pro-Russian group in the United States State Department with Alger Hiss as principal assistant. (Testimony before the House Committee on Un-American Activities, 8-30-48.)

Alger Hiss played a very important role in the formation of the United Nations. Hiss, a writer of the charter, was a convicted Communist spy who was drafted from a New York law firm, by Roosevelt's New Deal, in 1933. He joined the State Department in 1936. In 1944 Alger Hiss became the assistant director of the Office of Special Political Affairs which had charge of all postwar planning, most of which was directly involved in the creation of the United Nations. Even though his Communist involvement was widely known in March of 1945 he was promoted to the head director of that office.

It was this same Hiss who sat at Roosevelt's side at Yalta, and helped Joe Stalin get about everything he asked for, including three votes in the General Assembly of the United Nations. The United States has one. Roosevelt probably felt he was just throwing Stalin a "bone." He knew that Stalin was nothing more than a puppet on a string which was being pulled, from downtown New York City, the same place his string had been pulled for the past twelve years. Some believe that the big three at Yalta (Roosevelt, Stalin and Churchill) were all Masons.

Roosevelt's administration was satiated with Communists and one world globalist advisors and appointees. One was the likes of Harry Dexter White, the liaison officer between the Treasury Department and the State Department. He would later be sent to represent the United States along with Hiss and others in the formation of the United Nations, by Harry S. Truman. This was done even though Truman had information that White was a Communist.

There is no question that the Communists have been nothing more than well-fed puppets in the hands of the super-rich Masonic Illuminati Order of the trillionaire bankers. They have for the past century exploited the world for their own vain and devilish lusts. But, to witness one president after another use the power and authority of the office to commit one traitorous act after another against the Constitution of the United States, as well as, connive behind closed doors and stab the American people in the back, is almost beyond belief.

Since the United States joined the United Nations we have not won a war in which we have fought, except that trumped up affair in Iraq, and that was not considered an American war, but a war waged by the United Nations. It was purposely staged for the express purpose of furthering the "lamb-beast" government of the anti-Christ United Nations. Nothing of any significance goes on in this world without the sanction of the first and second beasts.

The merger of these two beasts is now so close that the United States cannot do anything militarily, without the full agreement of the U.N. Security Council, and the approval of the commanding general of the United Nations. As a rule, the commanding general of the United Nations has been Communist. It was agreed upon by the U.S. State Department in the beginning that a Soviet National would be given this strategic post in the U.N. (William Jasper, *Global Tyranny Step by Step* [Appleton, WI: Western Islands, 1992], 16, 17).

(In light of this, all Americans need to ask their senators why Bill Clinton is so eager to place our entire military under the Russian high command.)

When we look back to Korea it is not difficult to figure out why.

Harry S. Truman

The reason General MacArthur and Harry Truman had the problems they had was because, Truman was getting his directives from the U.N. Russian general as to what MacArthur could do or could not do. He was then passing it on to General MacArthur as his own personal strategies. When the truth finally came out, we see that the United Nations did not want the Americans to win in Korea, and Truman saw to it that we didn't. When the Chinese began to pour thousands of troops across the Yalu River, General MacArthur ordered the bridges to be bombed. Before the Air Force could carry out the orders, Washington issued new orders that the bridges were not to be bombed. General MacArthur in great disappointment stated, "I realized for the first time that I had actually been denied the use of my full military power to safeguard the lives of my soldiers and the safety of my army. To me, it clearly foreshadowed a future tragic situation in Korea and left me with a sense of inexpressible shock" (Charles A. Willoughby and John Chamberlain, *MacArthur, 1941–1951* [New York, NY: McGraw-Hill], 401, 402). The reason MacArthur could not use his full military power came straight from the U.N. charter.

> Article 1. The parties undertake, as set forth in the charter of the United Nations . . . and to refrain in their international relations from the threat or use of force in any manner inconsistent with the purposes of the United Nations.

> Article 4. . . . (military) measures taken under this paragraph shall be immediately reported to the security council of the United Nations. . . .

> In Korea, CFR insiders allowed the U.N. to dictate the "no-win" policies that guaranteed heavy losses of our soldiers and, ultimately, defeat. Secretary of Defense George Marshall admitted that the U.S. "hot pursuit" policy allowing our pilots to pursue attacking enemy aircraft back into their own territory was abandoned because the policy had failed to win U.N.

support. Secretary of State Dean Acheson stated: "There have been resolutions of the general assembly which make clear the course that the general assembly thinks wise; and the United States is endeavoring to follow the course which has tremendous international support and is not contemplating taking unilateral steps of its own."

Through the U.N., the communist forces were kept informed of "allied" military plans and operations. General MacArthur stated: "That there was some leak in intelligence was evident to everyone. (Brigadier General Walton) Walker continually complained to me that his operations were known to the enemy in advance through sources in Washington." General Mark Clark said: "I could not help wondering and worrying whether we were faced with open enemies across the conference table and hidden enemies who sat with us in our most secret councils."

Red Chinese General Lin Piao made this shocking admission: "I would never have made the attack and risked my men and military reputation if I had not been assured that Washington would restrain General MacArthur from taking adequate retaliatory measures against my lines of supply and communication." He knew the fix was in Washington. (William F. Jasper, *Global Tyranny . . . Step by Step* [Appleton, WI: Western Islands], 311, 312)

If that was the kind of traitorous cooperation our leaders were giving to the "enemy" over forty years ago, what do you think is going on today?

Alger Hiss was unofficially influential in the selection and employment of 494 of the United Nations initial staff members. The vast majority of these "Americans," were shown to be of the Communist ideology.

Dwight D. Eisenhower

When Dwight D. Eisenhower came to office in 1952 there was serious concern throughout Washington that the government of the United States, as well as, the "Americans" over at the United Nations needed to be purged of the enemies within. Eisenhower seemed to be the man for the job. He promised to clean house, but he never kept his promise. Not only were those who were great security risks kept on the job, many of them were highly promoted in the Eisenhower administration.

The Congress was trying to clean up the government, but Eisenhower stepped in, using the power of his office to interfere with the investigations by issuing an executive order, which later came to be known as the Gag Rule. This made it tremendously difficult to obtain information that Congress desperately needed.

The Bricker Amendment

The Bricker Amendment was designed to protect and safeguard our Constitution and Bill of Rights and keep them from ever being overridden by any treaty made with any government or governing bodies. When campaigning, Eisenhower pretended to favor such an amendment, but once elected, he made a complete about face and used every power at his disposal to defeat it. Since Eisenhower was a Republican, he was able to swing enough votes to defeat the amendment by one vote.

Today, the Constitution of the United States and the Bill of Rights hangs on its last thread. The undermining is complete. The traitors to this great declaration of freedom are coiled like a poisonous viper waiting for the opportune moment to strike. That grand document under which we have all slept in peace and partook of its great benefits, will very soon be snatched from us. This will happen because we used these great liberties not to glorify God, but to party and enjoy the pleasure of sin. "For her sins have reached unto heaven, and God hath remembered her iniquities" (Rev. 18:5).

In 1816 Thomas Jefferson wrote:

> The way to have good and safe government is not to trust it all to one, but to divide it among the many, distributing to everyone exactly the functions he is competent to handle. Let the National Government be entrusted with the defense of the nation and its foreign and federal relations; the state governments with the Civil Rights, laws, police and administration of what concerns the state generally; the counties with the local concerns of the counties; and each ward direct the interests within itself. It is by dividing and subdividing these republics from the great national one down through all its subordinations . . . that all will be done for the best. What has destroyed liberty and the rights of man in every government which has ever existed under the sun? The generalizing and concentrating all cares and powers into one body, no matter whether the autocrats of Russia or France or of the aristocrats of a Venetian senate. (Griffin, The Fearful Master [Belmont, MA: Western Island Pub., 1964], 19)

The Constitution of the United States guarantees that every state of the union would have a republican form of government within its constituted rights. But, the world court will have powers to meddle, to control, to manipulate, to decide what you may believe or not believe; the power to determine and judge even the sanity of any individual and make that determination in the light of their own criteria. They, will in time, choose whom you shall worship. They already have on the books at the United Nations thousands of laws and restrictions waiting to be fully implemented.

This beast which once in the eyes of the innocent had the appearance of a lamb, as John saw, now speaks with the voice of a dragon; in the not too distant future the world will have to submit to its every diabolical edict. This will come through the electronic computerized "mark," which in essence will be the covenant of control, that the United Nations will utilize to force each individual to conform to every law their dark mind might conceive.

All it will take to bring upon the American people this horrendous state of bondage is for the president to issue an executive order declaring that our government is bound by treaty to support and implement the world constitution of the United Nations. It will happen just that suddenly. It won't matter whether those behind the scene, such as the Federal Reserve System, create an emergency or blame a natural disaster. The Declaration of Independence will be trampled underfoot, and will be swallowed up by the lie of the ages. This will be the justified necessity used to transfer our military under the control of the United Nations; then perhaps United States soldiers will understand why they have filled out so many questionnaires relative to firing upon American citizens.

One survey required the following to be filled out by U.S. service men.

> I feel the president of the United States has the authority to pass his responsibilities as commander-in-chief to the U.N. secretary general.
>
> I feel there is no conflict between my oath of office and serving as a U.N. soldier.
>
> I would fire upon U.S. citizens who refuse or resist confiscation of firearms banned by the U.S. government. (John F. McManus, *Changing Commands* [Appleton, WI: Birch Society], 1, 2).

The above is an example of some of the questions which were asked of hundreds of U.S. Marines on 10 May 1994.

The World Court

When the United States became a member of the United Nations, it also became a member of the world court. But, the United States did not come under the actual jurisdiction of this court until it filed a formal declaration in the form of a United States Senate Treaty of Ratification. The American people were very fortunate to have had some senators who realized that the treaty would give the United Nations jurisdiction over the affairs of the United States. Instead of the United States Senate rejecting the treaty, they chose to add to Senator Morse's resolution, regarding matters which would be within the domestic jurisdiction of the United States, the words "as determined by the United States."

This one amendment is all that stands between the citizens of the United States and complete legal subjection to the paganistic schemes of the socialist world court. For several years there has been a continual effort in this country to generate support for the repeal of this amendment and the striking of those six words. The moment the American people, through its leaders, ever submit to the tribunal of the internationalists of the United Nations, we have forfeited our freedom to live and determine the future direction of our nation. But, as unthinkable as it possibly can be, the Bible says that we will commit that very act. America will give over its power to the United Nations. We see it clearly revealed in the words of the Apostle John. "And he (second beast) exerciseth all the power of the first beast before him" (Rev. 13:12).

Why should Americans ever be judged by the laws, and by people whom they have not chosen, to rule over them? So you, the citizens of America, may know who the enemies of your sacred liberties are, I shall name a few of those who have desired to appeal those six words: Dwight Eisenhower, John F. Kennedy, Richard Nixon, Adlai Stevenson, Dean Rusk, Lyndon Johnson, and almost every president since, especially the last one, Bill Clinton.

If you do not believe that these treaties have such power, consider the following remarks credited to John Foster Dulles, secretary of state in 1951.

> The treaty-making power is an extraordinary power liable to abuse. Treaties make international law and also they make domestic law. Under our constitution, treaties become the supreme law of the land. They are indeed more supreme than ordinary laws, for congressional laws are invalid if they do not conform to the Constitution, whereas treaty laws can override the Constitution. Treaties, for example, can take powers away from the congress and give them to the federal government or to some international body and they can cut across the rights given the people by the constitutional Bill of Rights. (Sen. William Jenner, *Congressional Record*, 83d Cong., 23 February 1954)

Maybe in the light of the foregoing we can understand the extreme push for "civil rights" worldwide which has been going on in the United States. I believe it is all "political conditioning" to cunningly deceive the United States Senate into a full ratification of the United Nations covenant on human rights. This would automatically replace our own Bill of Rights.

George Washington

We can see in the above statement of John Dulles the radical change which has come into the minds of the American leaders since joining the United Nations, in comparison to the kind of precious wisdom which was present when our country was founded. Compare the following words of Pres. George Washington with John Dulles.

> If, in the opinion of the people, the distribution or modification of the constitutional powers be in any particular wrong, let it be corrected by an amendment in the way in which the Constitution designates. But let there be no change by usurpation; for, though this in one instance may be the instrument of good, it is the customary weapon by which free governments are destroyed. (*American Historical Documents* [Washington, D.C.: Library of Congress], 144)

Yet, today among the Clintons we hear and witness such a different tune being played. To the present "globalists" the thinking of George Washington, Thomas Jefferson and Abraham Lincoln is too small for the world we live in today. Is that the truth or is that a lie they are preaching? The truth is, the Constitution of the United States was written in such a way as to prevent just such people as these "one worlders" from carrying out their diabolical schemes and enslaving the American people.

The Constitution and Bill of Rights were written as they were to harness or place great restrictions on what those in government could do. The presidents were and are answerable to the Constitution. But, since the days of Roosevelt, the presidents of the United States and every fraudulent group who selected them as the candidate for the office have been trying in every conceivable way to skirt and undermine this great document. The sad thing is that it appears that they are now putting the last nail in the board of a platform which totally circumvents the Constitution.

John F. Kennedy

It has been thirty years since John F. Kennedy was elected president of the United States. I still recall him taking his oath and swearing to uphold the Constitution of the United States. On 29 August 1961, Kennedy told the following to a group of students at the White House.

> After all, the Constitution was written under entirely different conditions. It was written during a period of isolation. It was written at a time when there were thirteen different units which had to be joined together and which, of course, were extremely desirous of limiting the central power of the government. That constitution has served us extremely well, but . . . it has to be made to work today in an entirely different world from the day in which it was written. ("President's Talk to the Student Interns," *New York Times*, 29 August 1962, 14)

The president of the United States should have said something to have encouraged those students to have had faith in what the Founding Fathers accomplished. The truth is the Constitution of the United States will work in any age or time in history. One does not have to find a way to make it work. But, Kennedy knew that the Constitution stood in the way of world government, and he cunningly planted the thought that it needed to be rewritten in those young minds.

Senator Fulbright

Let us listen to another United Nation's globalist from the state of Arkansas, Sen. J. William Fulbright, President Bill Clinton's dear friend and mentor.

> The president is hobbled in his task of leading the American people to consensus and concerted action by the restrictions of power imposed upon

him by a constitutional system designed for an 18th century Agrarian society far removed from the centers of world power. It is imperative that we break out of the intellectual confines of cherished and traditional beliefs and open our minds to the possibility that basic changes in our system may be essential to meet the requirements of the 20th century. (*San Diego Tribune*, 14 August 1961, B-1)

Two years later Fulbright stated that a "government by the people is possible but highly improbable, and that governments run by the elites is irrefutable insofar as it rests on the need for experience and specialized knowledge." When you listen to these guys you wonder how a farmer can know when he should plant his beans, or when a sinner should repent of sins. They are only satisfied when they can tell the farmer how many beans he can plant or what the teachers can teach in the local classroom. It is obvious that Fulbright did not believe that the American people were "bright" enough to govern themselves, and that some elite form of government should do it for them.

If people like Fulbright and President Kennedy thought that the Constitution was out of date, I wonder what they thought of the gospel of Jesus Christ which is nearing two thousand years in age, or the Ten Commandments which are over three thousand years old.

Today few of us realize just how far the Constitution has been spurned and trampled underfoot. Not only can treaties override our constitutional rights, but, also executive orders, personal agreements, and international pacts entered into by the president. Such agreements totally bypass Congress and sometimes are not even seen by the senate.

The Supreme Court in the *United States vs. Pink*, ruled, "A treaty is the law of the land . . . such interna-

tional compacts and agreements as the Litvinov assignment have similar dignity. . . . state law must yield when
it is inconsistent with, or impairs the policy or provi-
sions of a treaty, or of an international compact or
agreement" (Griffin, *The Fearful Master* [Belmont, MA:
Western Island Pub., 1964], 193).

The above reveals just how poised the first beast
(U.S.) is to transfer its power to the second beast (U.N.)
if and when a president of the United States chooses
to exercise an executive order enforcing the agreements which our country has made with the United
Nations. These orders will be final and there will be no
constitutional recourse to which we can turn.

How late it is, how far the night is spent; gross
darkness has gathered about out doors. We have been
led as lambs to a slaughter. Germany was a Christian
nation, it was inconceivable in the minds of those
German Christians, as well as, the world that such a
satanic system could suddenly manifest in their land.
Germany is a living tragic example of what is about to
be repeated in Christian America. Thousands of German Christians were not prepared for Hitler's regime
and submitted to his leadership and went along with
his atrocities whether they agreed or disagreed. Those
Christians who disagreed either were imprisoned, put
to death or fled for their lives. The Jewish people once
again are going to be put into this position along with
the Christians. The very death of our nation is imminent.

Sen. William Jenner

Forty years ago Sen. William Jenner declared: "The
United Nations is preparing a series of treaties which
operate as domestic legislation, affecting our citizens
in matters on which our Constitution does not permit
even our federal government to legislate. They would
abolish our Bill of Rights and replace it with a body of

state-granted privileges and duties modeled exactly upon the Soviet constitution" (Sen. William Jenner, "Amendment to the Constitution relating to treaties and executive agreements," Congressional Record, 23 February 1954).

Today, scores of new regulations are flooding our society placing new restrictions at all levels. What most of us have not known, is that these are laws being funneled down from the governing agencies within the United Nations.

J.B. Matthews, former chief investigator for the House Committee on un-American activities said, "I challenge the illusion that the U.N. is an instrument of peace. . . . It could not be less of a cruel hoax if it had been organized in hell for the sole purpose of aiding and abetting the destruction of the United States." Mr. Matthews could not have been more correct in his identification of where the inspiration came to form the United Nations. It was a plot conceived fundamentally by a group of men, of whose name you barely would dare speak above a whisper, according to President Woodrow Wilson.

The Two Horns of the Second Beast

"Superpowers as Super-partners . . . a new order . . . the United States and the Soviet Union, unite for crisis management around the globe" (*Newsweek*, 17 September 1990, 27).

The two most powerful entities which played the major role in the raising of this beast were Russia and the United States. These nations have been the mainstay of the United Nations, for without them the lamb could not have become as a dragon. There is no question in my mind that the United Nations is the second beast John saw rise up out of the earth, and the two horns which he saw upon his head could be none other than Russia and the United States. This beast needs only for the United States military to be turned over to its control, because Russia's military has long been available. Then he shall speak with the voice of a dragon (Rev. 13:11). This totalitarian government will take over the earth, and it has a constitution identical to the one of Communist Russia. A reign of terror and hell will then begin, and will spread throughout the whole earth. Whether Satan will ever put one man at the top, the world will have to wait and see. But, whether he does or not, we will not be able to stop this beast from becoming the most evil force that the world has ever seen.

William Jasper's recent book, *Global Tyranny . . . Step By Step*, states:

> America and the world stand on the brink of one of the most perilous epochs in this planet's history. . . . The true, imminent danger to America and to all nations seeking peace and goodwill stems from widespread acceptance of the monstrous falsehood that in order to live in an "interdependent" world, all nation-states must yield their sovereignty to the United Nations. This lie is given dignity by other lies, chief of which is that Soviet totalitarianism has been buried forever. (Introduction IX)

Those who know the hearts of the humanist "occult" Socialists are fully aware that these people are as anti-Christ as Hitler ever thought of being. The number of people that have been slaughtered by these socialist heathens, just since World War II is staggering. Where was the hue and cry from the United Nations when Stalin, Mao, and the rest of the Communist butchers were ridding the earth of millions and millions of the "unmentionables."

The answer is rather simple. The United Nations is a Communistic-Socialist creation who's innate philosophy has not changed. The elimination of a few million people here or there for the furthering of their agenda is to them socially and politically correct.

A New Coming World Religion

What is changing, is the strategy of Satan. We see entering into the minds of these Socialists, who once had no religion at all, the acceptance and participation in the demonic powers of the Eastern mystics. These powers revealed in Madame Blavatsky's theosophy of esoteric wisdom has become the accepted gospel through which the universal brotherhood of mankind, and the unity of all religions, can be attained.

The United Nations is gradually becoming the world leader of a syncretic new religion. The United Nations has become the "holy place" for dialogue, experimentation, and strategy for the purpose of unification and infusion of the religions of the world. In their thinking no one should be left out, rather all should with respectful tolerance and understanding be able to, in his own way, worship the same god together.

The present scheme of the second beast is bringing together the believers of Hinduism, Buddhism, Islam, Christianity, Taoism, mysticism, pantheism, atheism, communism, socialism, luciferian occultism, Jewish cabalist, masonism, and witch doctors into one common faith. The supreme magistrates of this new religion are already promoting their theological tenets on a worldwide scale. The religious leaders of the world have already undergone the preliminary phases of indoctrination.

This modern day tower of Babel will preach a gospel ranging from the worship of the environment, "mother earth," to occult ritualism. The involvement into the "new age of enlightenment" is sweeping the earth. Medicine is rapidly expanding and experimenting with various forms of occult rituals and power objects. New Age thinking, practices, and strategies are widely spreading throughout all of society. Even the New Age language and slang words can be heard coming from the mouth of the average person.

There is contained in the New Age philosophy an intolerant spirit very akin to the spirit of Communist dictators, and if this spirit is given opportunity to rule through a powerful political system, there will be no mercy spared for those who disagree with their agenda. There voice will shout loud and clear "crucify them, crucify them." In the beliefs of the more adept masters of the New Age movement they are convinced that the earth will need to be purged of all negative forces such as Bible believing Christians.

The United Nations is not only being praised as mankind's only hope for peace but as a divine messenger of God.

> We have meditations at the United Nations a couple of times a week. The meditation leader is Sri Chinmoy, and this is what he said about this situation: "The United Nations is the chosen instrument of God"; to be a chosen instrument means to be a divine messenger carrying the banner of God's inner vision and outer manifestation. One day, the world will . . . treasure and cherish the soul of the United Nations as its very own with enormous pride, for this soul is all-loving, all-nourishing, and all-fulfilling. (Donald Keys, President of Planetary Citizen)

Zeus

Today inside the United Nations building is a statue to their god Zeus. The ancient Greeks called him by this name. The Romans called him Jupiter. Jupiter was the king of all gods. He had no love or respect for his father Saturn and overthrew him. He heard a prophecy that his son would one day be wiser than he, so he ate him. The eating of his son gave him a headache, and the goddess Minerva sprang from his forehead fully robed in armor. He was a polygamist among the gods having many wives. He also had loved many mortal women. He was the father of Diana, Mercury, Mars, Perseus, Hebe Dionysys, and Hercules. He was also the god of thunder, lightning, and rain.

Jupiter is the god of the "rain." The prophet Daniel said, "I beheld even till the beast was slain, and his body destroyed" (Dan. 7:11). What is so extremely revealing is that the root meaning of the word "body" used in the above Scripture portrays the idea of a hard rain or a violent shower. Since Satan is the god of this world, Jupiter or Zeus would be one and the same as Satan. Then, what follows is that the beast and those marked by him will be worshippers of Zeus, and will therefore become saturated and soaked as it were in the violent outpouring of Satan's end-time spirit of death and deception. Thus, the body of the beast, the instrument of Satan, then becomes his vehicle through which he will violently manifest himself in this closing hour of world history.

It has become clear in my mind that when one partakes of "the mark of the beast" they will open their themselves to be saturated with the spirit of the false god Zeus (the powers of darkness). The Apostle John warned of the awful consequences to those who do.

> And the third angel followed them, saying with a loud voice, if any man worship the beast and his image, and receive his mark in his forehead, or in his hand,

> The same shall drink of the wine of the wrath of God, which is poured out without mixture into the cup of His indignation; and he shall be tormented with fire and brimstone in the pres-

ence of the Holy Angels, and in the presence of
the Lamb:

And the smoke of their torment ascendeth up
forever and ever: and they have no rest day nor
night, who worship the beast and his image,
and whosoever receiveth the mark of his name.

Here is the patience of the saints: here are they
that keep the commandments of God and the
faith of Jesus. (Rev. 14:9–12)

There is not much room for doubt that the United
Nations, the worshipper of Zeus, is the abomination of
desolation which is being set up to destroy the eternal
souls of men, and captivate as many of God's children
as is possible, and sweep them away into everlasting
damnation. The unification of all religions under the
religious affairs of this second beast that John saw will
bring about the creation of the greatest system of religion the world will ever witness. The stupendous hi-
erarchy of this great church is the false prophet the
Apostle John saw in his vision of the end (Rev. 16:13).
    Jesus said,

When ye therefore shall see the abomination of
desolation, spoken of by Daniel the prophet,
stand in the holy place, (whoso readeth, let him
understand:) *The holy place which is now emerging
in the eyes of the world is the United Nations.*

Then let them which be in Judea flee into the
mountains; let him which is on the housetop
not come down to take anything out of his
house:

Neither let him which is in the field return back
to take his clothes.

For then shall be great tribulation, such as was
not since the beginning of the world to this
time, no, nor ever shall be.

> And except those days should be shortened,
> there should no flesh be saved: but for the elect's
> sake those days shall be shortened. (Matt. 24:15–
> 18, 21–22)

Jesus is telling us, when you see the worship of
Zeus being made the official religion of the world, and
the "mark of the beast" set up, to flee society. Do not
try to hold on to the world. Forget it Jesus said, do not
even worry about your belongings. Jesus said flee to
the mountains. He may very well mean literal mountains, but he certainly means to flee with all our heart
unto the house of the Lord which is in the top of the
mountains. "Look," the psalmist said, "Unto the hills
from whence cometh your help."

Yes, God is going to cut short the reign of the
beast. For the bloodwashed believer it will last only
three-and-a-half years. Jesus said to watch and pray.
Watch for the merging of Russia and the United States
as the new army of the United Nations. When this
occurs, you will know that the time is short indeed
when abomination of desolations will be decreed.

John said,

> And I beheld another beast coming up out of
> the earth; and he had two horns like a lamb,
> and he spake as a dragon. And he exerciseth all
> the power of the first beast [U.S.] before him,
> and causeth the earth and them which dwell
> therein to worship the first beast [lick the hand
> of the first beast]. . . .
>
> And he causeth all, both small and great, rich
> and poor, free and bond, to receive a mark in
> their right hand, or in their foreheads:
>
> And that no man might buy or sell, save he that
> had the mark, or the name of the beast, or the
> number of his name. (Rev. 13:11–12, 16–17)

In Review of the Second Beast

1. The second beast would exercise all the power of the first beast before him. This is being fulfilled before our very eyes, as the presidents continue to by-step Congress, and yield the sovereignty of America into the hands of the supervision of the United Nations.

2. The image which John portrayed was one of a lamb. The image of the United Nations will continue to appear as a harmless creature, until full power and authority is given unto it, then fire will begin to proceed out of its mouth. John says this beast will speak as a dragon.

3. John foretold that the second beast would have two horns. Horns in Bible prophecy represent nations or kings. The United Nations' administration is saturated with Communists from top to bottom.

The unification of Russia from a political and military purpose is nearly complete. The only thing that I can think the United Nations might be hesitant about, in respect to Russia, is that many Americans cannot envision Russia as a peace keeper. But, since the political elite have sold the world on the fall of communism, then certainly "all is well" with the Soviets, in the eyes of most Americans.

The two horns of the beast are just about to reach their place of maturity and take their military position together, to be utilized as the brain of the beast would so desire. These two horns upon the same beast would give this monstrous dragon in sheep's clothing the most awesome array of power and authority this world has or will ever see. The two horns of the same beast, are the United States of America and the "United States of the Soviet Union."

On 11 September 1990, George Bush stated over national television, "Out of these troubled times, our fifth objective—a new world order—can emerge—we are now in sight of a United Nations that performs as envisioned by its founders." Not one patriotic American was among those who were selected to draft the charter and Constitution of the United Nations. Several of them were later found to be Communist spies and Communist sympathizers.

There was prophecy given back in the early forties, which said, "there are men and women in the government of the United States, which will in time rise to bite the hand that fed them."

All of the above will occur after the United States, the first beast, gives its power unto the second beast, the United Nations. Then the abominable kingdom of Satan, along with his demonic hoards, will have seized the human support necessary to take the world into the "nightmare" of history.

Chapter Eight

The Final
Offering of the
Great and Last Sacrifice

The prophet Daniel tells us that in the middle of the seventieth week the sacrifice and oblation will cease. "And he shall confirm a covenant with many for one week: and in the midst of the week he shall cause the sacrifice and the oblation to cease" (Dan. 9:27). The sacrifice and oblations of the old covenant ceased in the eyes of God when Jesus was crucified upon the cross. For anyone to seek to reestablish the old sacrifice of the shedding of the blood of bulls and goats for the remission of sin would be an abomination in the sight of God. For a nation, even if they are called by the name of Israel, could bring upon themselves the worst kind of desolation if they sought to trample again upon the blood of God's Son.

The angel Gabriel most certainly is not making any reference to a return to the blood of animals. He knew that when the time of the end arrived there would only be one blood sacrifice which would carry the seal of God. He knew the old covenant would have passed away.

If the Jews ever start slaughtering animals again for the purpose of the remissions of sins, it will not be under the direction of heaven. It would only be one more stench that would precede up from this earth into the nostrils of God.

The spirit of God will always agree with Himself when it comes to the impartation of the Word of God. This final week of the day of the Lord will focus only upon the blood of God's Son, and of His great and last sacrifice which He made upon the cross of Calvary.

To appreciate the prophecy which Gabriel gave to Daniel let us turn to the revelation of the Apostle Paul.

> Wherefore when he cometh into the world, he saith, sacrifice and offering thou wouldest not, but a body hast thou prepared me:
>
> In burnt offerings and sacrifices for sin thou hast had no pleasure.
>
> Then said I, lo, I come (in the volume of the book it is written of me,) to do thy will, O God.
>
> . . . He taketh away the first, that He may establish the second. (Heb. 10:5-7, 9)

The second sacrifice which God established was once, for all, and forever. In my mind I could not imagine a more dangerous act that the Jews could commit, than attempting to set up the old sacrifice and oblation.

The Apostle Paul continues to reveal the new and perfect "will" of God.

> By the which will we are sanctified through the offering of the body of Jesus Christ once for all.
>
> And every priest standeth daily ministering and offering oftentimes the same sacrifices, which can never take away sins:
>
> But this man, after he had offered one sacrifice for sins for ever, sat down on the right hand of God. (Heb. 10:10-12)

Jesus said, "And this Gospel of the kingdom shall be preached in all the world for a witness unto all nations: and then shall the end come" (Matt. 24:14).

In the above Scripture Jesus made it very clear that the gospel of His blood sacrifice would be offered at the time of the end, and it would be witnessed and verified unto all nations. Daniel told us that God would make a special covenant with many for one week, (the seventieth) which would distinctly be related to the "remission of sins," the sacrifice and oblation (Dan. 9:27).

This covenant will be made with those who hear the call and will have previously yielded to the necessary sanctification. We, as Christians, have known what God's Word expects from us. The Apostle Paul gives us one example.

> I beseech you therefore, brethren, by the mercies of God, that ye present your bodies a living sacrifice, holy, acceptable unto God, which is your reasonable service. And be not conformed to this world; but be ye transformed by the renewing of your mind, that ye may prove what is that good, and acceptable, and perfect, will of God. (Rom. 12:1)

This assignment will require a faith to leave all, and go as the Spirit leads with a warning voice to the inhabitants of the earth. This may be in your own city or county, but it may be to the furthermost corner of the earth. I believe when this trumpet sounds in the realm of the Spirit there will come the deepest conviction of sin that the Body of Christ has ever felt. This will begin I believe on the first day of the seventh month (Tishri) and will continue being felt until the end of the tenth day. The tenth day is the day of atonement or judgement, Yom Kipper (Lev. 23:27–32). God said judgement would begin at His house. At this time God will judge those who are ready and willing to abide this "double portion covenant" of the Elijah ministry, and become His frontline warriors and battle axes to thrash the nations and prune His vineyard for the last time.

I believe it will become a burning desire within us to be a witness for Jesus and to no longer keep the light under the bushel. The desire to warn and plead with the souls of men will possess our thoughts continually. I believe this Spirit of God will cause our heart, as David said, to pant after God as the hart does after the water brook (Ps. 42:1).

The Feast of Tabernacles (Lev. 23:34–44) begins just five days later and lasts for seven days. I believe that on the first day of this feast, the mighty anointing of God's Spirit will start to move upon His chosen ones. For seven days He will be "searching out the hearts of men before His judgement seat" for the purpose of making them fishers of men. For three-and-a-half years the Gospel will shake the nations as a tree in a mighty wind.

The Apostle John beheld in vision the awesome anointing which will accompany these chosen ones as they move through the nations proclaiming with a loud voice, "Repent for the hour of judgement is come." John wrote, "And I will give power unto my two witnesses, and they shall prophesy a thousand two hundred and threescore days, clothed in sackcloth" (Rev. 11:3). The clothing of sackcloth tells us that these servants will be ministering in the purity of the spirit. Their ministry will not portray the image and pseudo-characteristics of the many popular ministries we have witnessed for the past thirty or forty years.

I believe this end-time fire of God will begin as a spark in a forest and will gradually spread, increasing in power and in demonstration as the weeks go by. Perhaps, much like the picture which is given in Daniel of the "stone" cut out of the mountain without hands, which continued to roll until it became a great mountain, and filled the whole earth (Dan. 2:34–35).

I believe the two witnesses John testified of are a prophetic similitude. God has, since the beginning, established His Word by the mouth of two or more witnesses. When Jesus sent out "the seventy," He had called them two by two. These two witnesses reveal that same divine administration of the kingdom, that He will do again in the last invasion of the nations. Jesus said, "For where two or three are gathered together in my name, there am I in the midst of them" (Matt. 18:20). And again, "In the mouth of two or three witnesses every word may be established" (Matt. 18:16).

The same will be with the witnesses of this hour as it was with Jesus. In due time the very demonstration of the power and the spirit will announce their coming and going. It will be a challenge for some of those who are in the plush and popular ministries to step "down" into this sackcloth calling of God. But, they can, if they forget those things which are behind and look forward to things which are set before.

I believe there is a great company waiting out there in the world that God has been preparing, who will thrust in their sickle and reap with all their might while the day lasts. I believe many of those that will be called are already doing great, but unadvertised, exploits in places, which many of us would be unwilling to go. The world in time will be amazed at this bold phenomenon, which they will see and hear in the lives of so many young and old, male and female.

This invasion of God will be made up of servants and handmaidens whose commitment will be as flint, and whose testimony will in time strike fear into the hearts of the hardened and rebellious. These servants of the Most High will create a great awakening to the awesome reality of God and will cause millions to be swept into the kingdom of God.

The prophet Joel foretold the coming of this mighty army of God. His testimony is vividly pictured in physical activity, but to understand what God is revealing, it is necessary to meditate upon his vision before we can fully appreciate its spiritual uniqueness.

> Blow ye the trumpet in Zion, and sound an alarm in my holy mountain: Let all the inhabitants of the land tremble: for the day of the Lord cometh, for it is nigh at hand;

> A day of darkness and of gloominess, a day of clouds and thick darkness, as the morning spread upon the mountains: a great people and a strong; there hath not been ever the like, neither shall be any more after it, even to the years of many generations.

> A fire devoureth before them; and behind them a flame burneth: the land is as the garden of Eden before them, and behind them a desolate wilderness; yea, and nothing shall escape them.

> The appearance of them is as the appearance of horses; and as horsemen, so shall they run. Like the noise of chariots on the tops of mountains shall they leap, like the noise of a flame of fire that devoureth the stubble, as a strong people set in battle array.

> Before their face the people shall be much pained: all faces shall gather blackness.

> They shall run like mighty men; they shall climb the wall like men of war; and they shall march every one on his ways, and they shall not break their ranks;

> Neither shall one thrust another; they shall walk every one in his path: and when they fall upon the sword, they shall not be wounded.

> They shall run to and fro in the city; they shall run upon the wall, they shall climb up upon the houses; they shall enter in at the windows like a thief.

The earth shall quake before them; the heavens shall tremble: the sun and the moon shall be dark, and the stars shall withdraw their shining:

And the Lord shall utter His voice before His army: for His camp is very great: for He is strong that executeth His word; for the day of the Lord is great and very terrible; and who can abide it? (Joel 2:1–11)

We can see in natural language the awesome anointing as it empowers and strengthens this end-time army to move unchecked and relatively unchallenged against the forces of darkness. The world will witness a complete demonstration of God's authority, and if they reject it, there will be little hope of escaping the wrath which is to come. God gives us a very clear picture of the extensive authority of this anointing that will roll out of the mouth of His people. "And I will give power unto my two witnesses, and they shall prophesy a thousand two hundred and three score days" (Rev. 11:3).

Their testimony will be one continual spirit of prophecy for three-and-a-half years. This is telling us that God, by the power of the Holy Spirit, through His servants and handmaidens is explaining to the inhabitants of the earth exactly what is coming.

These witnesses will be warning the world not only of the devil's trap to eternally damn their souls, but, also of the coming wrath of God upon the unrepentant. It will be their testimony of the truth which shall so anger the hearts of those who have covenanted with Satan to ensnare the world. Great anger will be spawned by their testimony.

Their witness will, also, be directed toward the socially minded Christians, who are sliding into the most deceptive sellout to the devil since the Fall of Adam. The gospel will be preached with such clarity that no one will be confused over the message they proclaim.

John writes, "And if any man will hurt them, fire proceedeth out of their mouth, and devoureth their enemies: and if any man will hurt them, he must in this manner be killed" (Rev. 11:5). This kind of preaching is a whole lot different than what is presently going on today. I've heard of several churches and pastors who packed up and moved their congregation when Satanists began to put "curses" upon them.

But, this army will walk in the white light of the power of the Blood of Jesus, and their words will be with fire and the Holy Ghost. I am not going to waterdown what John saw. I believe he knew what fire looked like; one thing for sure, Elijah did. Nevertheless, the Bible records that Ananias and his wife Sapphira fell in the face of such judgment (Acts 5:1–11). This army will have power to shut heaven, "That it rain not in the days of their prophecy: and have power over waters to turn them to blood, and to smite the earth with all plagues, as often as they will" (Rev. 11:6).

Notice the words, "as often as they will." When we are under the anointing of the Holy Spirit's power, our desires and wills are surrendered to God. We then respond to what His desire or will might be.

We see in this prophecy the kind of anointing that is upon these covenant witnesses. John is describing both the mantles of Moses and Elijah combined into one as resting upon them. The white light of this witness will leave the world without excuse. "Every mouth may be stopped, and all the world may become guilty before God" (Rom. 3:19).

But, while this great witness is being proclaimed, Satan will send forth his army of counterfeiters. For three-and-a-half years the most cunning and deceiving preachers and prophets will arise under the anointing of Satan to try and counteract this witness of God. The rider on the white horse will be galloping at full tilt in every sector of society.

For 1,260 days this witness will shake the nations, and I have to believe that during those three-and-a-half years God will reap His greatest harvest. The angel revealed to John that those who would come out of the Great Tribulation would be, "a great multitude, which no man could number, of all nations, and kindreds, and people, and tongues" (Rev. 7:9).

These attacking saints of God will be labeled as fanatical religious extremists and false prophets, with all their miracles labeled as some diabolical form of sorcery. But, in spite of all the lies that hell can manufacture, millions will be plucked from the everlasting fire.

Then at the end of those three-and-a-half years a trumpet will be heard in the realm of the spirit; it will be the voice of the commander-in-chief speaking to His army. He will give the order, "It is finished, the Gospel has been preached unto all nations, and the appointed time has come that the sacrifice and oblation spoken of by Daniel the prophet will cease."

This will happen in the middle of the week. Just as suddenly as it all had begun three-and-a-half years earlier, it will just as suddenly cease. The day and the time will be the same as when Jesus said, "It is finished," there that day upon the cross, "In the fourteenth day of the first month at even is the Lord's Passover" (Lev. 23:5). Sometime in late March or early April at the end of 1,260 days the Lord will call His troops from the battlefield.

The battle will have been furious, but the world will have been reaped. The lukewarm Christians will have had three-and-a-half years to make up their minds as to whether they really want to be identified with the hated, the persecuted, and the tried. Jesus said either you are for or against me, there will not be any middle ground when He makes up His jewels. The lukewarm, He will spew as it were out of His mouth (Rev. 3:16).

There will have been such intense pressure of every kind to stop the servants of God, that when Jesus does cut off the preaching of the Word of His Blood, the demonically deceived minds of the earth will believe that they have won. The Apostle John writes, "And when they shall have finished their testimony, the beast that ascendeth out of the bottomless pit shall make war against them, and shall overcome them, and kill them" (Rev. 11:7). But, notice the beast had to wait until they had finished their testimony, before he could perform the most diabolical intents of his heart.

This time everything will come out into the open, the true spirit and attitude of the world will be revealed. The world's reaction will be witnessed on television. God's servants will be smeared in every beastly controlled newspaper and magazine in the world. Before the allotted days come to an end, the devil and his crowd will become insane with anger. But, they will not stop the preaching of the gospel, until He who restraineth is taken out of the way (2 Thess. 2:7). That will not come until the gospel witness is finished.

This witness of the gospel will cover exactly the same length of time as did the ministry of Jesus, and with greater works than those that He did. When it is over, the wheat will have been separated from the chaff. All Christians will have to carefully examine the ground upon which they stand at this very dangerous time lest they should fall. It is sad to say, but many "Christians" will become offended at this witness, and they will join in with the world in their renunciation of God's true servants. How tragic, indeed, will it be when the deceived learn the truth.

Toward the end of the three-and-a-half years the Satanic attack will escalate to all-out condemnation. Laws will be passed. Many will be thrown in jail, but, the jails will not hold them. The plans and snares of the enemy will be revealed far in advance. The demonically controlled governments will become desperate in their efforts to stop the witness. Many will be the occasion when the servants of God will pass through the midst of those who would arrest and charge them.

In the midst (middle) of the seven years, Jesus will cause the sacrifice and oblation to cease. The nets will be full. Satan's anger will be boiling over, and his anger could very well be reflected in the quick finalization of setting up the "numbering system." Shortly after these three-and-a-half years the world government will have accomplished the closing of all churches, making the public preaching of such a gospel unlawful throughout the world.

In God's wisdom I can see His allowing the banning of the preaching of the Blood of Jesus to closely coincide with His command to cease the preaching of His vicarious sacrifice. The beastly system of the world will interpret it as one of the great social victories of all time; an exhilarating celebration enjoined between demons and humans. This celebration will break out all over the earth. The world will not cease to gloat and rejoice over their imagined "victory" for the next three-and-a-half years. The ministry to the Body of Christ will continue, and the closing of churches will cause the wicked to believe that they at last had power over the ultraconservative Christians. But in all appearances the witness of the gospel, as far as the world is concerned, will lie dead in the streets of this end-time Sodom and Egypt world, where and for whom our Lord was crucified (Rev. 11:8).

I believe that Jesus had us in mind when He told His disciples, "Verily, verily, I say unto you, that ye shall weep and lament, but the world shall rejoice: and ye shall be sorrowful, but your sorrow shall be turned into joy" (John 16:20).

The thorn in their side will have been removed and now they are free at last to go as far to the "left," and as deep into the darkness of rebellion against God as their heart would desire. It is very clear from verse 7 that God is permitting the beast liberties which he did not appear to have the first three-and-a-half years. Now the beastly world government will be able in any locale to make prime examples for all the world to behold. Where before it appeared to be impossible to kill the witnesses, until they had finished their testimony as it was with Jesus, now the possibility exists as it did with Jesus.

Although, any laying down of lives will be strictly to fulfill God's own purposes, as John reveals.

> And when he had opened the fifth seal, I saw under the altar the souls of them that were slain for the Word of God, and for the testimony which they held:

> And they cried with a loud voice, saying, How long, O Lord, holy and true, dost thou not judge and avenge our blood on them that dwell on the earth?

> And white robes were given unto every one of them; and it was said unto them, that they should rest yet for a little season, until their fellowservants also and their brethren, that should be killed as they were, should be fulfilled. (Rev. 6:9–11)

The beast's rise to power as seen in Revelation 11:7 is more clearly understood in Revelation 13:5, 7 where we read: "And power was given unto him to continue forty and two months (3½ years). And it was given unto him to make war with the saints, and to overcome them." The prophet Daniel wrote that the horn (beast) would wear out the saints of God and that many would be purified, and made white, and tried, and the time of great trial would take place within the 1,290 days.

We see in both Revelation 11:7 and 13:7, that the beast would, "make war against them," and "make war with the saints." John in chapter 13 makes it clear who the two witnesses are. They are the saints. Also, in chapter 13, we see the beast rising to power for forty-two months. This is three-and-a-half years. This clarifies the symbolism of three-and-a-half days in chapter 11 where the saints or witnesses will be overcome.

The root word to "kill" in Revelation 11:7 is separate or cessation, which helps us to understand what will happen when the "mark" and the severe attack comes upon the saints. Their activities will cease as they are separated from society, the beast already will have outlawed God's people from television, radio, and from holding meetings in promotion of the gospel.

When my daughter, Robin, was very young she had a dream where she saw a train going across the country and evil men were collecting books and Bibles from the Christians. I don't believe we have too long to wait before the religious affairs committee of the United Nations will come out with "their" approved authorized version of the Bible. Then in due time the law will go forth from the "almighty religious elite" of the institute of Zeus in New York City, which will outlaw all other versions.

When the preaching and teaching of the gospel has finished and the believers are removed from society, then He that had restrained the evil one, the Holy Spirit, will be removed also (2 Thess. 2:11). When the removal of the Holy Ghost occurs, then the earth will plunge deep into the depths of the most deceptive forms of cruelty, evil, and darkness. This fall, I believe, will begin immediately after the Lord calls His servants from the harvest fields. The world will speedily ripen for destruction. Satan will have his own unrestrained license to take them into the depths of his depravity.

For the night will have come when no man can work (John 9:4). The work and ministry of the Holy Spirit will, for the next three-and-a-half years, distinctly focus His attention upon the Body and Bride of Christ. The Bride to be will enter into a place with God that few upon this earth have ever known.

Chapter Nine

The Bride
Shall Overcome

The prophet Daniel revealed that the saints of God would be given into the hands of the beast for three-and-a-half years. "And he (the beast) shall speak great words against the Most High, and shall wear out the saints of the Most High, and think to change times and laws; and they shall be given in his hand until a time (1 year), and times (2 years), and the dividing of time (½ year)." We find the second witness of this given by John in Revelation 13:5, "Power was given unto him to continue forty and two months." The Christians who have been chosen to follow "the Lamb" during these 1,260 days or three-and-a-half years will enter into a time of trial of which there will be no hope of over-coming, except by the sustaining power of the Blood and Word of the Lamb of God (Rev. 12:11).

Every individual within organized society will, during this period of time, bow their knees to the beast and name his name. Or, by faith, as did Lot, walk out of Sodom and not look back. Those that do will be obeying the admonition given by the Apostle John. "And I heard another voice from heaven, saying, come out of her, my people, that ye be not partakers of her sins, and that ye receive not of her plagues" (Rev. 18:4).

Those that make up the Bride of Jesus will be required to prove their love, devotion, and faithfulness for forty-two months. This last half of Daniel's seventieth week will bring everything to a head. The Christian during these three-and-a-half years will experience the revelation of what God has called him to become. He will experience the fulfillment of the prayer which Jesus prayed in the seventeenth chapter of the Gospel of John, saying that our hour had come, and we will be sanctified through the word of truth, and by that sanctification we will be made perfect in one.

In the midst of this perfecting fire the Bride will travail as a woman about to be delivered.

> A woman when she is in travail hath sorrow, because her hour is come: But as soon as she is delivered of the child, she remembereth no more the anguish, for joy that a man is born into the world. And ye now therefore have sorrow: But I will see you again, and your heart shall rejoice, and your joy no man taketh from you. (John 16:21–22)

The Church will, during this period of time, travel through the deepest valley of sorrow. Jesus said we would be delivered up to be afflicted, and some of us will die for Him, and all nations shall hate us. The Bride of Jesus is going to be deeply persecuted. But, by the grace of God, she will not only overcome the fear of death, but during these forty-two months will, by the Blood of Jesus through God's almighty resurrecting power, defeat death itself and put it once and for all under her feet.

With the coming of the "mark of the beast" the temperature of the furnace of persecution will continue to increase until the true believers will be driven totally from the world into a dependence upon Jesus they have never known before. There in the depths of that great dependency, Jesus will impart unto us the glory of His life. Gradually we will be brought into the full realization of what the Apostle Paul preached centuries ago to the saints at Galatia. He testified, "I am crucified with Christ: Nevertheless I live; yet not I, but Christ liveth in me: and the life which I now live in the flesh I live by the faith of the Son of God, who loved me, and gave Himself for me" (Gal. 2:20).

This great transformation can only take place after we are spewed out by the world. We will cease to be enjoined to the world for any sustenance of life. As we face that trial of separation from the world, we will need to have a firm grip upon a faith that will not shrink and will not tremble on the brink of any earthly woe. That's the kind of faith Paul was testifying of, where we lay the world aside and we "run with patience the race that is set before us, looking unto Jesus the author and finisher of our faith; who for the joy that was set before Him endured the cross, despising the shame" (Heb. 12:1–2).

We will have no other choice but to consider Him that endured such contradiction of sinners against Himself, lest we become wearied and faint in our minds (Heb. 12:3). The beast shall overcome many because of that very thing. For a few days we must be chastened (tried in the fire) after the pleasure of God's will; this for our profit, that we might be partakers of His Holiness (Heb. 12:10).

Thus, in due time, we will shake off every fetter and influence of the world that had bound us, and lose even the appetite for things we once so deeply cherished. A spirit of contrition and submissiveness will take hold of our hearts, enabling us to experience more powerfully the working of the word of truth within and upon us, even as it did when its power worked upon the ground to form Adam from the dust. God's loving kindness will undertake for us as it did for the

Israelites under Moses, but on a far deeper scale as it divides and separates us molecule by molecule from the Adamic curse. "Wherefore, as by one man sin entered into the world, and death by sin; and so death passed upon all men" (Rom. 5:12).

The last three-and-a-half years, the "Bride to be" of Jesus will be "made ready" in the womb of tribulation prepared by God. There the spirit of the world will lose its controlling hold and influence upon the saints. The Bride, in the midst of that time, will have the veil removed off her soul and will experience a full sanctification at the feet of God's glory, which will birth her into the sinless likeness of her Lord.

This will fulfill the will of God as preached by the Apostle Paul, "that He might sanctify and cleanse it with the washing of water by the Word, that He might present it to Himself a glorious church, not having spot, or wrinkle, or any such thing; but that it should be holy and without blemish" (Eph. 5:26–27).

As the forty-two months nears its completion, the glory of Jesus will be revealed in her. She will come forth as pure gold. The Bride will enter spirit, soul, and body into the righteousness of Christ. The Word will have become meat and drink indeed. The furnace of the government of the beast will have become God's daily boiler room where purity of the spirit and soul will be forged. The Bride's affections and attachments to the present world will vanish away, and her heart will become fixed upon the kingdom of God. She will literally, as the Scriptures testify, gaze so steadfastly upon Jesus that she will be changed into the same image from glory to glory, by the Spirit of the Lord (2 Cor. 3:18).

In due time her spiritual beauty will be reflected in her clothing of light, her desire to be clothed upon with her house which is from heaven will be heard with groanings which cannot be uttered.

For we know that if our earthly house of this tabernacle were dissolved, we have a building of God, an house not made with hands, eternal in the heavens.

For in this we groan, earnestly desiring to be clothed upon with our house which is from heaven:

If so be that being clothed we shall not be found naked.

For we that are in this tabernacle do groan, being burdened: not for that we would be unclothed, but clothed upon, that mortality might be swallowed up of life. (2 Cor. 5:1-4)

As the eyes of the Bride become single to God's glory her whole body will be filled with light (Matt. 6:22). The Bride will reach such depths of faith and revelation that she will draw from the Holy Spirit the full realization of the desires of her heart. In that kind of faith God will withhold no good thing from her, for it will be clearly understood that it is the Father's good pleasure to give unto the Bride of His Son all things that pertain to life and godliness within His kingdom.

She will then, in due time, as she eats the flesh and drinks the Blood of her Saviour, attain unto the resurrection of the dead; and as it was the great heart's desire of the Apostle Paul that the full power of the cross could be made manifest in his life, so shall it be with the Bride. He wrote, "That I may know Him, and the power of His resurrection, and the fellowship of His sufferings, being made conformable unto His death; if by any means I might attain unto the resurrection of the dead" (Phil. 3:10-11).

Paul tells us, "For since by man came death, by man came also the resurrection of the dead" (1 Cor. 15:21). The great victory will have been won at last. The Bride of Christ will have entered into the full

force of the redemptive power of Calvary. She will fully
understand that all Adam lost in the Fall was won and
again made available to her through the death and
resurrection of Jesus. The Bride will fully awaken to
this truth, and will rise into the kind of faith that will
please God, and will lay claim to all that Jesus had
bought for her through His Blood.

Dear reader, we will soon understand and enter
into that like faith of Enoch, which the Scriptures testify, "by faith Enoch was translated that he should not
see death; and was not found, because God had translated him: for before his translation he had this testimony, that he pleased God" (Heb. 11:5). During these
three-and-a-half years there will come a desire in the
heart of each of us to please God. Our entire beings
will cry out with the most powerful emotion, until our
whole life will be possessed with the desire to please
our Lord and our God. This great unified cry, coming
from every part of the globe where the saints can be
found, will in time rend the heavens and bring the Son
of God down.

"Even we ourselves groan within ourselves, waiting
for the adoption, to wit, the redemption of our body"
(Rom. 8:23). That manifestation will occur at the conclusion of three-and-a-half years of the most intense
spiritual crushing at the wine press of God which He
specially prepared for the Bride's perfection. For, at
that time, the awesome power of death, which has
disfigured God's creation since the beginning, will be
overcome. Mortality will put on immortality and mortality will be swallowed up of life (2 Cor. 5:1).

The Apostle Paul tells us, "Wherefore, as by one
man sin entered into the world, and death by sin; and
so death passed upon all men, for that all have sinned"
(Rom. 5:12). The last enemy that shall be destroyed is
death. But, death has to be destroyed in the physical
bodies of God's people through the resurrection power

of the Holy Ghost. The Church thus far has been in such darkness that the light of this knowledge has been unable to shine unto them. But, this light will brightly shine in the midst of the coming tribulation.

The prophet Isaiah presents a good description of the coming of this breakthrough. "Arise shine; for thy light is come, and the glory of the Lord is risen upon thee. For, behold, the darkness shall cover the earth, and gross darkness the people: but the Lord shall arise upon thee, and His glory shall be seen upon thee" (Isa. 60:1).

The Apostle Peter reveals to us that Jesus must remain in heaven until the times of the restitution of all things. "Whom the heaven must receive until the times of restitution of all things, which God hath spoken by the mouth of all His holy prophets since the world began" (Acts 3:21). The Apostle Paul helps us to understand this restitution.

> For I reckon that the sufferings of this present time are not worthy to be compared with the glory which shall be revealed in us. For the earnest expectation of the creature waiteth for the manifestation of the sons of God. For we know that the whole creation groaneth and travaileth in pain together until now. And not only they, but ourselves also, which have the first fruits of the spirit, even we ourselves groan within ourselves, waiting for the adoption, to wit, the redemption of our body. (Rom. 8:18–19; 22–23)

No part of creation can be restored until the head of that creation, you and I, make that final and full response to God. That response, in turn, will give God the liberty to release the healing redemptive power necessary to remove the curse of Adam from all of creation. The end cannot come until Jesus has put down all rule, all authority, and all power, for He must reign (from heaven) until He hath put all enemies under His feet. The last enemy that shall be destroyed is death (1 Cor. 15:24–26).

This defeat of the enemy will be accomplished within, as we move deeper and deeper into the Blood of our Saviour. God has placed into the Blood of Jesus His resurrection power. The devil knows that, and that is the reason why he has focused his attack upon the Blood of the gospel since its inception. He has been able to turn our attention from the blood and cloud our understanding of its awesome power. This unfathomable power of the blood is nowhere more clearly revealed than in the Scripture which testifies of Jesus being resurrected by the means of His own Blood. "Now the God of peace, that brought again from the dead our Lord Jesus, that great shepherd of the sheep, through the blood of the everlasting covenant" (Heb. 13:20).

It shall be no different for us. We will by faith lay hold of the blood, and will drink it from morning till evening until the blood is transfused into our spirit, soul, and body. Death will lose its grip and fade away in the presence of the glory of the Blood of the Lamb. Then will be fulfilled the Scripture, "They overcame him by the blood of the lamb, and by the Word of their testimony" (Rev. 12:11).

We think we sing songs about the blood now, but the day is coming when everyone of us will know that without the blood we will not survive, not even one day. Then the blood will become so precious, and will hold meaning so deep that words cannot tell. The wonder of its glorious truth will touch the deepest emotion of our hearts. The Blood of Jesus will then draw so near to our souls, and its tender goodness will wrap its loving arms about us. Then we will begin to comprehend the power that is in the blood, and as we do, the Spirit of God will take us into the bosom of its love and holiness. The veil will part and we will then understand that the Blood of the Lamb is the "river of life" which has been flowing to us from out of the "heart of God." Then we will sing with all our soul and our heart and strength,

> There is a fountain filled with blood
> Drawn from Emmanuel's veins;
> And sinners plunge beneath the flood
> Lose all their guilty stains
>
> Dear dying lamb, thy precious blood
> Shall never lose its power
> Till all the ransomed Church of God
> Be saved to sin no more
>
> E'er since, by faith, I saw the stream
> Thy flowing wounds supply,
> Redeeming love has been my theme
> And shall be till I die.

The blood will be our refuge in this coming dark hour. It will be the strength of our faith. The blood will be our covering and the peace to our souls. The blood will hold back the invading demons bringing every conceivable curse and disease. The blood will nourish not only our spirit and our soul, but the blood will feed our body, as well as, keeping it fit and whole. Yes, we will sing nothing but the Blood of Jesus, "nothing but the Blood of Jesus."

The reason that many of the Corinthian saints had failed to discern the Lord's body was because their faith in the blood had vanished from their hearts. The apostle said, "For this cause many are weak and sickly among you, and many sleep" (1 Cor. 11:30). But, those who are not appointed to death at the hands of the beastly system, will only survive as they flee by faith into the sanctuary of the Blood of the Lamb.

The prophet Daniel helps us to see what God is doing within His people at the time of the end. "Many shall be purified, and made white, and tried; but the wicked shall do wickedly: and none of the wicked shall understand; but the wise shall understand" (Dan. 12:10).

The end cannot come until Jesus delivers up the kingdom to the Father and until He has put down all rule and authority. "Then cometh the end, when He shall have delivered up the kingdom to God, even the Father; when He shall have put down all rule and all authority and power. For He must reign, till He hath put all enemies under His feet. The last enemy that shall be destroyed is death" (1 Cor. 15:24–26).

Jesus, also, said that at the time of the end all things that offend would be rooted out of the kingdom. All Christians need to remember is that nothing offends God more than fear and unbelief. Those two things make it impossible for God to help us. "The son of man shall send forth His angels, and they shall gather out of His kingdom all things that offend, and them which do iniquity; then shall the righteous shine forth as the sun in the kingdom of their Father. Who hath ears to hear, let him hear" (Matt. 13:41, 43). This will be the time of the foolish virgins (Matt. 25:2–12). There will be no place to hide as the Holy Spirit perfects the Bride.

The end is conditioned by the kingdom. When the kingdom of God has fully come, His people will have come into the purity of the spirit, and will be fully clothed upon with the love of God. The curse will loosen its grip upon their bodies as the resurrection power of God is made manifest in their mortal flesh. Then cometh the end, even the manifestation which heaven and earth has waited these long six thousand years. The time of the prophesied mystery is ready to be revealed.

The rapture of the Bride of Christ cannot occur as long as Satan has legal rights to the physical bodies of the saints. When Adam fell, death passed upon all men, thus causing mortality (death) to enter the flesh, as well as, the spirit. When man's spirit is void of the life of God, he automatically falls prey to the manipulative power of darkness. Thus, in short order, he will take on Satan's nature of pride and greed.

This total separation from the world will enable the Bride to undergo a special transmutation in the power of God. She will experience the fire of God's love to the degree that she will be able to say, as did her Lord to His persecutors: Father forgive them for they know not what they do. The temptation to seek to save her life will have no place. She will have entered deep into the understanding of the Apostle Paul.

> According to my earnest expectation and my hope, that in nothing I shall be ashamed, but that with all boldness, as always, so now also Christ shall be magnified in my body, whether it be by life, or by death.

> For to me to live is Christ, and to die is gain.

> But if I live in the flesh, this is the fruit of my labour: yet what I shall choose I wot not.

> For I am in a strait betwixt two, having a desire to depart, and to be with Christ; which is far better. (Phil. 1:20-23)

The Bride will know the end is near and that Jesus will soon come for her. This clear knowledge will draw her heart out into the purest praise and worship to the deepest depth of intimacy as her heart embraces the groom in the purest of love. Then, the full glory of the cross will manifest in the lives of every true and faithful worshiper. The Apostle John understood the transformation which would occur when such hope matured into a living faith. "Beloved, now are we the sons of God and it doth not yet appear what we shall be: but we know that, when He shall appear, we shall be like

Him; for we shall see Him as He is. And every man that hath this hope in him purifieth himself, even as He is pure" (1 John 3:2–3).

Faith will reach perfection. Jesus will be her all in all. This faith of the Bride will please God as did Enoch of old, and nothing can be withheld from her. A beautiful birth into the realm of God's pure and holy light will come toward the end of the three-and-a-half years. The suffering in many ways will have been so intense, that many will have laid down their lives for their love of Jesus (Rev. 6:9). But, through it all, the Bride comes forth as pure gold. The burning fire of the Lord's pure love will have done its perfect work.

The revelation of the Holy Spirit will be given line upon line until the perfecting wisdom of God permeates every thought. Heaven will draw so very near to the saints of God. Angels will be ministering to them daily. They will love not their lives even unto death. What the apostle understood, so shall they, that whether they live or die makes no difference.

The heart of the Bride will be possessed, to walk in the will of God in perfect obedience. Even the smallest of details will become so very significant. She will be yielded at last. During these three-and-a-half years the saints will come to understand how God and His Word are one. So many times in years gone by, Christians have carelessly treated God's Word, being ignorant that it is a living substance of spirit and life (John 6:63). But, as the Word becomes fully engrafted within her heart the glory of its divine power will become hers to enjoy. The Bride will know that she is eating of that Tree of Life which once stood in the midst of Eden's garden.

For three-and-a-half years the wicked will have rejoiced believing that Bible Christianity is finally silenced in all the earth. But, as Daniel said, "None of the wicked shall understand" (Dan. 12:10). They could not perceive that they were the furnace in the hands of God, and were operating within the bounds of God's own discretion.

As the three-and-a-half years comes to a close, it is obvious that the enemies of God will not realize that their defeat is imminent. They will not understand what the Bride of Christ has achieved, and that through her great overcoming through the Blood of the Lamb, the Father will turn to Jesus and say, "Son, it is time to go to receive the hand of your Bride." The world will be completely taken by surprise, they will not have the slightest awareness that the glorious victory and awesome manifestation of the first resurrection is about to shake the earth.

When the Bride comes out of the closet, arrayed in the white linen of God's immortal light, then the enemies of God will witness a sight of shocking proportion. They will scream with fear and flee for somewhere to hide. Jesus will at the same time step into the earth's atmosphere. Heaven will depart as a scroll when it is rolled together; and every mountain and island will move out of their place (Rev. 6:14). Men of all stations in life will hide themselves from the face of Him that's appearing in the sky.

Tremendous rejoicing will break forth in heaven as the announcement is made: "Let us be glad and rejoice, and give honour to Him: for the marriage of the Lamb is come, and His wife hath made herself ready" (Rev. 19:7). The time for the unveiling of the mystery of God has come.

Just before the opening of the seventh seal the Apostle John writes, "And I saw another angel ascending from the east, having the seal of the living God: and he cried with a loud voice to the four angels, to whom it was given to hurt the earth and the sea, saying, hurt not the earth, neither the sea, nor the trees, till we have sealed the servants of our God in their

foreheads" (Rev. 7:2–3). This sealing is just before the
rapture takes place. The last one has been prepared.
The time has now come for the angel to put the trumpet to his mouth.

This is the final trump which will sound complet-
ing Daniel's seventieth week. The sounding of this last
trumpet will fulfill the prophecy given to the Apostle
Paul:

> Behold, I shew you a mystery; we shall not all
> sleep but we shall all be changed, in a moment,
> in the twinkling of an eye, at the last trump: for
> the trumpet shall sound, and the dead shall be
> raised incorruptible, and we shall be changed. So
> when this corruptible shall have put on
> incorruption, and this mortal shall have put on
> immortality, then shall be brought to pass the
> saying that is written, death is swallowed up in
> victory? O death, where is thy sting? O grave,
> where is thy victory? The sting of death is sin;
> and the strength of sin is the law. But thanks be
> to God, which giveth us the victory through our
> Lord Jesus Christ. (1 Cor. 15:51–52, 54–57)

Complete victory over sin, death, and the devil in
spirit, soul, and body, will be attained in the face of all
that the devil could throw at God's people. She will by
the grace of God have told the devil, the beast, and all
the hosts of this world that Jesus is all she needs. Then
she will walk out of the world and into the valley of
martyrs and will have proven to both demons and
man, that greater was He that is in her than he that was
in the world (1 John 4:4).

When the angel from the east cries with a loud
voice it will be as the sound of a mighty trumpet to be
heard around the earth. Jesus described it thus, "And
he shall send His angels with a great sound of trumpet,
and they shall gather together His elect from the four
winds, from one end of heaven to the other" (Matt.
24:31).

Paul declared it with even more detail:

> For the Lord Himself shall descend from heaven with a shout, with the voice of the archangel, and with the trump of God: and the dead in Christ shall rise first: then we which are alive and remain shall be caught up together with them in the clouds, to meet the Lord in the air: and so shall we ever be with the Lord. (1 Thess. 4:16–17)

The Apostle John revealed that at the end of the three-and-a-half years or prophetic days, "The spirit of life from God entered into them, and they stood upon their feet; and great fear fell upon them which saw them" (Rev. 11:11–12).

The Bride of Christ has put on the heavenly garments arrayed in the glorious light of God. Without question, she is clothed upon with the same "fine linen" of divine light which had clothed our first parents in the garden.

The spiritual victory for which Jesus had died almost 2000 years ago was now won. Death was now defeated. The enemy of man, which had for six thousand years stalked the human family and had plagued the world with sorrow, had been dealt his fatal blow (Heb. 2:14–15). The mystery is revealed. The Bride instantaneously is clothed upon with her body from heaven. But, she did not gain this great eternal victory just for herself, but for all those who had gone on before and were waiting for the redemption of their bodies. For as the Scriptures testify, "that they without us should not be made perfect" (Heb. 11:40).

Instantly the next wonder occurs, the ground begins to rumble—graves throughout the whole world begin to open—all who had died in Christ return to receive their bodies as the angel sounds. His trumpet is heard by the saints as "a great voice from heaven saying unto them, come up hither. And they ascended up to heaven in a cloud; and their enemies beheld them" (Rev. 11:12). The rapture of the Bride has finally come. It was not done in secret but out in the open where the whole world witnessed God keeping His word of promise. "And if I go and prepare a place for you, I will come again, and receive you unto myself; that where I am, there ye may be also" (John 14:3). The saints had overcome by the Blood of the Lamb, and by the word of their testimony (Rev. 12:8)!

The Apostle John was told to write, "Blessed are they which are called unto the marriage supper of the Lamb" (Rev. 19:9).

> And one of the elders answered, saying unto me, What are these which are arrayed in white robes? And whence came they? And I said unto him, Sir thou knowest. And he said to me, These are they which came out of great tribulation, and have washed their robes, and made them white in the blood of the Lamb. (Rev. 7:13-14)

I believe the rapture will occur near the time of Rosh Hashanah and the Feast of Tabernacles in the Jewish month of Tishri. The seventieth week of Daniel will conclude at that period of time. It appears that the saints could be in heaven until the time of Passover. It was just after Passover that the final judgment fell upon Pharaoh and his army. It was at the time of Passover that the judgment of the world fell upon Jesus. I believe the judgment will fall upon the beast and his armies at or near the time of Passover in the valley of Armageddon and simultaneously upon the rest of the world. This means that the Bride would be in heaven for seven months, which would be for the entire duration of the wrath of God as it is poured out upon the world. The Bride will be returning with Jesus at the time of the annihilation of the armies of the beast (Rev. 19:14).

The following song was written by one whose heart burns with the love of Jesus. I have never met a person more precious. She has given her life to the adorning of the Bride throughout the nations of the earth.

His Bride Has Made Herself Ready

His bride has made herself ready, as she sweeps thru the portals above,
Arrayed in shining fine linen, her heart filled with God's perfect love.

Chorus:

(Be glad and rejoice and give honour, for the marriage of the Lamb is come.
His bride has made herself ready, adorned in glory and love.)

She is gathered from out of all nations, washed in the blood of the Lamb,
Transformed in His image and likeness, to rule and reign with Him.

Chorus:

Behold, she is the King's daughter, her garments are wrought of fine gold;
Their needlework tells of her suff'ring; 'tis the greatest love story e'er told.

Chorus:

Blessed are they who are called, to the marriage supper of the Lamb;
All heaven has waited this hour, when she's ushered unto His right hand.

Chorus:

(Gwen Shaw, ETH, Inc.)
The music for this song may be obtained from:
End-Time Handmaidens, Inc.
P.O. Box 447
Jasper, AR 72641

Chapter Ten

The
Battle of Armageddon

The prophet Daniel tells us that from the time the daily sacrifice shall be taken away and the abomination that maketh desolate is set up, there shall be 1,290 days or three years and seven months (Dan. 12:11). This would be thirty days past the ending of Daniel's seventieth week. Since the Rapture occurs very near the end of the seventieth week, this tells us that the Bride of Christ will have been in heaven for thirty days when this final abominable act will be ready to be executed. The "mark of the beast" will at this time have been in operation for over three-and-a-half years. Therefore, the actual worship or "licking the hand of the beast," is not the final abomination which will bring desolation to the beastly system.

Sometime in the fall of the year 2003, the patience of the beast will run out for the nation of Israel. She has refused to bow the knee and give up her sovereignty as a nation and unite with the world in spite of every kind of political and economic pressure the beast could bring against her. What many have forgotten about the Jewish people and their history is that many of them will die before they will bow to the worship of a heathen God.

Satan's snare to capture the hearts of the Jewish people in Israel has failed. He now lays out his final

plans through the beast and the false prophet to bring
about Israel's annihilation. These plans for Israel's complete destruction are not only in harmony with the
"new age" doctrine of eliminating the "unfit"; but,
reveals the full wrath of Satan which he has held in his
heart against the ancient covenant people since he
learned that God chose them to be the carrier of the
oracles of God until the Messiah was revealed.

The entire world will manifest a hatred toward
Israel that will far surpass the horrifying spirit of Hitler
during World War II. The only safety for the Jew at
this time, in all the world, will be in the land of Israel.
God says in His Word that by the time this heinous act
is ready to be committed against the Jew, He will have
gathered them back into their own land, and will have
"left none of them any more there" (Ezek. 39:28). God
knows that every Jew in the world will have been butch-
ered except He gather them back under the feathers of
His wings, in the land of their fathers.

It is very interesting to read in the great vision of
John in the Book of Revelation just how the plans were
initiated for the assembling of the nations of the earth
against Israel.

> And I saw three unclean spirits like frogs come
> out of the mouth of the dragon, and out of the
> mouth of the beast, and out of the mouth of
> the false prophet. [Demonic inspiration and
> collaboration taking place between the United
> Nations, and the heads of the religious affairs
> of the world church.] For they are the spirits of
> devils working miracles, which go forth unto
> the kings of the earth [ten regions] and of the
> whole world, to gather them to the battle of
> that great day of God Almighty. (Rev. 16:13–14)

It is of interest to note that during the reign of
ancient Babylon (594 B.C.–524 B.C.) God moved upon
the prophet Ezekiel to prophesy of the great battle of

Armageddon to be fought during the reign of the end-time Babylon. Many have interpreted Ezekiel's prophecy as basically a Russian confederation coming against Israel as a separate battle altogether from the Battle of Armageddon. But a close analysis of John's prophecy in Revelation with Ezekiel's prophecy will reveal they are one and the same.

The Apostle John reveals that Gog and Magog are symbolic of the entire earth (Rev. 20:8). Here we read that Satan after the millennium "shall go out to deceive the nations which are in the four quarters of the earth, Gog and Magog." Therefore, from the Bible we learn that Gog and Magog are representative of the whole earth.

Magog was a son of Japheth. Japheth was Noah's first born son, and it was primarily from his seed that eastern and western Europe came. This would, also include the United States. Today, we see a great mixture of Ham, Shem, and Japheth spread throughout the earth. Ezekiel gives an excellent description of who the people are that will assemble at the Battle of Armageddon. He begins by naming the sons of Japheth: Magog, Meshech, Gomer, and Tubal. He then writes of Persia, Shem's descendants. Then of Ethiopia, and Libya's descendants of Ham. He then further expands upon the seed of Japheth and Gomer, and all his bands, Togarmah of the north quarters and all his bands and many people with thee (Ezek. 38:1–6).

The beast of Revelation will gather his bands also from the kings of the whole earth (Rev. 16:14). We find the prophet Zechariah is in full agreement.

> Behold, I will make Jerusalem a cup of trembling unto all the people round about, when they shall be in the siege both against Judah and against Jerusalem. and in that day will I make Jerusalem a burdensome stone for all people: all that burden themselves with it shall

be cut in pieces, though all the people of the
earth be gathered together against it. (Zech.
12:2–3)

When we understand that both the United States
and Russia are fully committed to the New World Order,
then it is simple to conclude that this army of which
the prophets are speaking is the new army which will
be operating under the flag of the second beast. This
is one reason why all nations are pictured as Gog and
Magog.

The army that Ezekiel saw was so large that he
could only describe it as a "cloud to cover the land,"
a great company, a mighty army (Ezek. 38:15–16). We
find the Apostle John putting a number to this "cloud
which covers the land." "And the number of the army
of the horsemen were two hundred thousand thousand: and I heard the number of them" (Rev. 9:16).
Two hundred million soldiers would certainly be a
cloud which would cover the land. The size of this
army will cover the entire valley of Meggiddo, and
beyond.

The military orders will go out to the kings of the
earth during the time of the sixth angel, and by the
time they are all gathered together there in the valley
of Megiddo, the seventh angel will be loosed. "And the
seventh angel poured out his vial into the air; and
there came a great voice out of the temple of heaven,
from the throne, saying, it is done" (Rev. 16:17). The
time of the great supper of God has come (Rev. 19:17).

The invading armies will apparently bring great
suffering upon Israel before the Lord steps in to save
the remnant of His people.

> For I will gather all nations against Jerusalem to
> battle; and the city shall be taken, and the houses
> rifled, and the women ravished; and half of the
> city shall go forth into captivity, and the residue

of the people shall not be cut off from the city. Then shall the Lord go forth, and fight against those nations, as when He fought in the day of battle. (Zech. 14:2-3)

As the collective armies of the United Nations attack Israel, a great earthquake occurs. John tells of this earthquake happening at the time of the Battle of Armageddon. "And He gathered them together into a place called in the Hebrew tongue Armageddon. . . . And there were voices, and thunders, and lightnings; and there was a great earthquake, such as was not since men were upon the earth, so mighty an earthquake, and so great" (Rev. 16:16, 18).

Ezekiel associates this quake with the awesome presence of God.

Surely in that day there shall be a great shaking in the land of Israel; so that the fishes of the sea, and the fowls of the heaven, and the beasts of the field, and all creeping things that creep upon the earth, and all the men that are upon the face of the earth, shall shake at my presence, and the mountains shall be thrown down, and the steep places shall fall, and every wall shall fall to the ground. (Ezek. 38:19-20)

As the presence of the Lord is shaking the earth, the Lord is seen in the heavens with all the saints and angels. Great derision breaks out among the armies below and seemly without reason they commence fighting each other. Ezekiel says, "Every man's sword should be against his brother" (Ezek. 38:21).

The prophet Zechariah testifies of the same thing happening. "And it shall come to pass in that day, that a great tumult from the Lord shall be among them; and they shall lay hold every one on the hand of his neighbor, and his hand shall rise up against the hand of his neighbor" (Zech. 14:13). It appears that the whole earth will be filled with war and killing.

Thus, as the Battle of Armageddon ensues, the Lord will rain upon the armies great hailstones, fire, and brimstone (Ezek. 38:22). John writes, "And every island fled away, and the mountains were not found. And there fell upon men a great hail out of heaven, every stone about the weight of a talent; and men blasphemed God because of the plague of the hail; for the plague thereof was exceeding great" (Rev. 16:20–21).

No prophet drew a more candid picture of what the multi-national forces of the beast will experience than did the prophet Zechariah. "And this shall be the plague wherewith the Lord will smite all the people that have fought against Jerusalem; their flesh shall consume away while they stand upon their feet, and their eyes shall consume away in their holes, and their tongue shall consume away in their mouth" (Zech. 14:12). Many have described this as atomic warfare, but, I personally believe the prophets who have written that God will smite them with the breath of His own mouth. The Bible tells us that our God is a consuming fire.

The prophet Isaiah describes the Lord whose tongue is a devouring fire, and whose breath is like a stream of brimstone (Isa. 30:27, 33). The Apostle John describes Jesus preparing to leave heaven for the Battle of Armageddon as one whose eyes were as a flame of fire, and out of His mouth goeth a sharp sword, that with it He should smite the nations (Rev. 19:12, 15). I cannot find in Scripture where Jesus is in any way going to be dependent upon or utilize the carnal weapons which men have designed to fight this great end-time battle.

The Apostle John writes, "And the remnant were slain with the sword of him that sat upon the horse, which sword proceeded out of his mouth" (Rev. 19:21). The Lord will speak the same all-powerful Word in the end of the world to destroy, as He did in the beginning when He made it all.

Ezekiel and John both agree that the armies of the beast will be given to the ravenous birds of every sort, and to the beasts of the field, to be devoured.

And, thou son of man, thus saith the Lord God: speak unto every feathered fowl, and to every beast of the field, assemble yourselves, and come; gather yourselves on every side to my sacrifice that I do sacrifice for you even a great sacrifice upon the mountains of Israel, that ye may eat flesh, and drink blood. Ye shall eat the flesh of the mighty, and drink the blood of the princes of the earth. (Ezek. 39:4, 17–18)

John so vividly describes the same:

And I saw an angel standing in the sun; and he cried with a loud voice, saying to all the fowls that fly in the midst of heaven, come and gather yourselves together unto the supper of the great God; that ye may eat the flesh of kings, and the flesh of captains, and the flesh of mighty men, and the flesh of horses, and of them that sit on them. (Rev. 19:17–18)

From the above we learn that atomic warfare was not used to destroy these men. If it had been, the radiation would have contaminated their flesh, as well as the whole area, thus killing the fowls and making it impossible for such a feast to physically take place. Sometimes Bible scholars forget that God is in full charge of this battle, and absolutely nothing will transpire unless He permits it. There in the valley of Armageddon 166 million soldiers of the beast will die as the prophet says, one-sixth will be left alive. "And I will turn thee back, and leave but the sixth part of thee, and will cause thee to come up from the north parts, and will bring thee upon the mountains of Israel" (Ezek. 39:2).

The beast will have certainly planted his military tabernacle, a tent clearly conspicuous, between the seas and will come to his end there in the valley of Megiddo and none shall help him (Dan. 11:45). In Daniel 11:40, just before Satan attacks Israel, tidings out of the north and east shall trouble him. Satan will know that the tumults in the sky are the war drums of God. He will know that the commander-in-chief of the armies in heaven is on the way. Therefore, He will order the armies of the beast to attack. "But tidings out of the east and out of the north shall trouble him: therefore he shall go forth with great fury to destroy, and utterly to take away many" (Dan. 11:44). Perhaps Michael will be coming out of the north and Jesus from the east (Matt. 24:27). It will be a time of awful trouble as little Israel can only be saved by her Messiah King.

The defeat of the beast ushers in the millennial reign of Christ and the setting up of His house and throne in Jerusalem. The world will know that Jesus Christ is Lord and King. It is interesting to note that both in Ezekiel and Zechariah that the Lord has to confirm among His own people Israel, that He is the Lord their God. "The house of Israel shall know that I am the Lord their God from that day and forward" (Ezek. 39:22).

Perhaps the Jews need to reread the word of the prophets, even their own prophets reveal that they do not know their God, for they are declaring that they must yet come to know Him.

Armageddon will have brought to a head all the strife and every murderous intention of the devil. The last few months upon the earth will have been a "nightmare." The time of trouble and tribulation will have passed and the darkness will have been dissolved in the brightness of the Lord's coming. The glory of the Lord will move to fill the earth and the healing of the nations will begin.

It is a good feeling to finally reach the twentieth chapter of Revelation where John tells us of the things which transpire immediately following the Battle of Armageddon. We read:

> And I saw an angel come down from heaven, having the key of the bottomless pit and a great chain in his hand.
>
> And he laid hold on the dragon, that old serpent, which is the devil, and Satan, and bound him a thousand years,
>
> And cast him into the bottomless pit, and shut him up, and set a seal upon him, that he should deceive the nations no more, till the thousand years should be fulfilled: and after that he must be loosed a little season.
>
> And I saw thrones and they sat upon them, and judgment was given unto them: and I saw the souls of them that were beheaded for the witness of Jesus, and for the Word of God, and which had not worshipped the beast, neither his image, neither had received his mark upon their foreheads, or in their hands; and they lived and reigned with Christ a thousand years.
>
> But the rest of the dead lived not again unto the thousand years were finished. This is the first resurrection.
>
> Blessed and holy is he that hath part in the first resurrection: on such the second death hath no power, but they shall be priests of God and of Christ, and shall reign with Him a thousand years. (Rev. 20:1–6)

The United Nations and its Satanic leadership will go one step too far when they think the evil thought to totally destroy the nation of Israel, and to wipe the Jew from the pages of history. God had cut a covenant with

Abraham which was to last through all generations. The world will tragically learn that the covenant God made in blood with Abraham (and eventually mixed it with His own blood at the cross) was a pact so strong that not only will it bring down the evil empires of the devil, but, it also brings an end of six thousand years of death and sorrow as it rips Satan himself from off the throne of this world.

The prophet Zechariah who had made that first journey back to Jerusalem with Zerubbabel when King Cyrus of Persia released the captives in 524 B.C., concludes that day with these words: "And the Lord my God shall come, and all the saints with thee" (Zech. 14:5). (Those who have had problems understanding whether or not the saints were raptured need to read again what the prophet just said.) That is exactly in agreement with the prophecy of Enoch.

"And Enoch also, the seventh from Adam, prophesied of these, saying, Behold, the Lord cometh with ten thousands of His saints, to execute judgement upon all" (Jude 14–15).

Continuing with Zechariah,

> And it shall come to pass in that day, that the light shall not be clear, nor dark: but it shall be one day which shall be known to the Lord, not day, nor night: but it shall come to pass, that at evening time it shall be light. And it shall be in that day, that living waters shall go out from Jerusalem; half of them toward the former sea, and half of them toward the hinder sea: in summer and in winter shall it be. And the Lord shall be king over all the earth: in that day shall there be one Lord, and His name one. (Zech. 14:6–9)

> And His name shall be called Wonderful, Counsellor, the Mighty God, the everlasting Father, the Prince of Peace. Of the increase of His

government and peace there shall be—no end, upon the throne of David, and upon his kingdom, to order it, and to establish it with judgment and with justice from henceforth even for ever. (Isa. 9:6-7)

But in the last days it shall come to pass, that the mountain of the house of the Lord shall be established in the top of the mountains, and it shall be exalted above the hill; and people shall flow unto it.

And many nations shall come, and say, Come, and let us go up to the mountain of the Lord, and to the house of the God of Jacob; and He will teach us His ways, and we will walk in His paths: for the law shall go forth of Zion, and the word of the Lord from Jerusalem. (Mic. 4:1-2)

Chapter Eleven

"I Am Come for Thy Words"

One of the great revelations in the Bible is found in the Book of Daniel. The angel is speaking to the prophet Daniel, "Fear not, Daniel: for from the first day that thou didst set thine heart to understand, and to chasten thyself before thy God, thy words were heard, and I am come for thy words" (Dan. 10:12).

A dear Christian friend of ours had a dream not too long ago. It is as follows:

> In the dream I saw my husband and I walking across a bridge or what seemed to be a bridge. It was the type you would see in the jungles. It was strung from one high place to another over a deep valley. The part that you actually walked on was made of a white material, it looked like styrofoam.

> My husband was walking in front of me single file. We were holding on real tight to the rails. As I looked from side to side, I could only see the tops of what looked like bushes and tops of trees. The bridge was moving up and down with the swells of water. I, also, noticed that the water was a dirty brown. I believed that the Lord revealed to me that this was a bridge over troubled waters, an unclean time in the world in which we were passing through.

My husband and I continued across this bridge
and when we got to the end of it there was a
room there. We went into the room and I saw
a book and it was open. I picked up the book
and written across the top of the page was,
"Daniel," in black letters. Written in scripture
form were the words, "I weep and mourn at
Daniel's feet" in red letters. I remember thinking, "I wish there were more notes." (Karen
Endsley)

There are many valuable notes in the Book of
Daniel. The meaning of some of them were greatly
considered in this book. There is no question that
Daniel's words carried great power with God. There
are yet many things which all of us can learn at the feet
of Daniel in this last hour. The reason this is so, is
because God gave Daniel a word for those who were
appointed to perform His work at the time of the end.
The above dream was shared with me just a few days
before this book went to the printers.

Oh, that we may be like Daniel and chasten ourselves before God, that our words may be those which
God will come for. How important it is that the words
we speak will be like Daniel's, as well as, those of the
prophet Samuel, which was written of him, "and Samuel
grew, and the Lord was with him, and did let none of
his words fall to the ground" (1 Sam. 3:19). When God
is able to treat our words the way He does His own,
then when the word goes out of our mouth which we
have spoken, it shall not return unto us void, but, it
shall accomplish the thing where unto it was sent (Isa.
55:11).

I believe the average Christian has never given much
consideration as to whether his words are falling to the
ground or whether they are being taken by angel's
hands into the throne room of God. I have met few
people who are disciplined with their words, to the

extent that they are concerned whether or not they are pleasing the Lord with all the words that come out of their mouths.

As we prepare for the coming "end of the world" and the tremendous spiritual battles which lay before us, we will need to give serious heed to the counsel of the Bible and examine ourselves to see if we are walking in the faith once delivered unto the saints.

One sure way of giving the "spirit of this world" an advantage over us is not to watch the words we live by. Jesus made sure He watched His. He answered the devil and said, "It is written, man shall not live by bread alone, but by every word that proceedeth out of the mouth of God" (Matt. 4:4). One of the most vital functions of living by the Word of God is to make sure that we stay in agreement with the Word.

Salvation directly corresponds to what we say and what we believe (Rom. 10:10–11). God reaches our minds by the word of truth. It is when our minds perceive this truth, and we desire to experience that which it tells us, then God can bring it to pass in our life. The Apostle Paul continues in that same chapter to reveal to us that faith comes by hearing the Word of God. It is as we hear the Word of God that we develop within our hearts the kind of faith which will please God. The hearing of the Word affects the way we think and speak. It is the language of both our hearts and mouth which greatly concerns God.

Jesus said this concerning the words that we speak, "that every idle word that men shall speak, they shall give account thereof in the day of judgment. For by thy words thou shalt be justified, and by thy words thou shalt be condemned" (Matt. 12:36–37).

The prophet told Israel, "Take with you words, and turn to the Lord: say unto Him, take away all iniquity, and receive us graciously: so will we render the calves of our lips" (Hos. 14:2). The prophet is exhorting us to offer unto God the first expressions of what we have to say. Many times the first thing which comes out of a person's mouth looses the devil and not the angel of God. Sometimes we have to offer a sacrifice of praise in the presence of our enemies, in the midst of pain, disappointment and evil reports.

The apostle wrote that you have not because you asked not. Jesus said that you ask and you shall receive, for it is the Father's good pleasure to give to you the kingdom of God; that by our words we shall be condemned or by our words we shall be justified. God made man to commune with Him, and it would be through that communion that God would give to man all things that pertained to life and godliness. His path was to be filled with light and his heart satisfied with the riches of his God.

The Apostle James wrote that the prayer of a righteous man availeth much. The righteous man will pray a prayer of faith, when he has made God's Word his own and boldly affirms the promise that it declares as his own. Jesus told us in Mark 11:22–23 that we had to talk to our mountain (need). If you are going to remove a mountain with machinery, you have to stay on the job until the mountain is leveled. That mountain could be a multitude of things, ranging from sickness to a crop in the field. We are to take His name and speak to those things just as if Jesus would, if He were standing in our shoes.

I recall speaking to a man about his air conditioner in his automobile on a very hot Sunday afternoon. I asked him as I was standing beside his car and the family perspiring within, "Isn't your air working?" He said, "It's out and it's going to cost several hundreds of dollars to fix it; it's all shot." He had just paid for my family's lunch. I said, "Open the hood." He did. I said, "Put your hand on that air conditioner, with me." I spoke a simple word of faith to the air conditioner. I said, "I command you in the name Jesus to produce cold air." We put the hood down and I told my friend, to get into the car, start it up and turn on the air. I will not describe his amazement as the cool air began to flow into his car. It seems at times my faith rises more quickly to help others with their mountains, than it does with my own. I think the problem with that is that we become too lenient with our own mountains.

When we began to speak to our mountains, first off it pleases God, because that is what Jesus told us to do (Mark 11:23). But, it also pleases Him because that is the way that He operates. He spoke the worlds into existence. He expects us to do the same with the world with which you and I are responsible for.

There are angels of God, abiding with all the saints of God, who are eager to do great exploits for the believer. But, they must wait for words, righteously spoken words of faith, specifically directed by the desires of our heart. When our desires are "kingdom" desires, the more intense will our faith become and we will wax bold, confident, and possess great assurance within our hearts. God is watching such words from our hearts with great attentiveness. His spirit will anoint such words because they agree with Him. The Apostle Paul told Timothy, "Hold fast the form of sound words, which thou has heard of me, in faith and love which is in Christ Jesus" (2 Tim. 1:13). Such words the angels await to receive. Angels will not take just any kind of word that is spoken out of our mouth, only words of love, faith, and blessing.

The Apostle James writes, "But let him ask in faith, nothing wavering. For he that wavereth is like a wave of the sea driven with the wind and tossed. For let not that man think that he shall receive any thing of the Lord" (James 1:6–7).

The angels of God discern whether words spoken have come out of a heart ruled by faith. For David of old wrote concerning the angels, "Bless the Lord, ye His angels, that excel in strength, that do His commandments, hearkening unto the voice of His Word" (Ps. 103:20). Again, in the Book of Hebrews, we read concerning the work of the angels, "And of the angels He saith, . . . ministering spirits, sent forth to minister for them who shall be heirs of salvation?" (Heb. 1:7, 14).

When we establish our hearts in the truth of what God's pure Word declares, then the words we speak will arise out of a soil of righteousness unmixed with the vain imaginations of unbelief. The word of faith can only have as its foundation the truth of God's Word. Words which do not agree with the "word of faith" will bind the hand of God on our behalf. Simply because, that which is not of faith is sin (Rom. 14:23).

Jesus showed us the way into the heart of faith. "If ye abide in me, and my words abide in you, ye shall ask what ye will, and it shall be done unto you" (John 15:7). That is, love Him, worship Him, do all we do in His name. The Church is yet to comprehend the power of the name of Jesus in their hearts. The Scriptures tell us, "And whatsoever ye do in word or deed, do all in the name of the Lord Jesus, giving thanks to God and the Father by Him" (Col. 3:17).

Jesus assures us that the words we will then speak will move heaven and the angel will surely come for our words. Jesus did not stop there. He went on to reveal the effect that our walking in this kind of faith would have upon our Father in heaven. "Herein is my Father glorified, that ye bear much fruit; so shall ye be my disciples" (John 15:8). Jesus told the Jews that were believing in Him that, "If ye continue in my Word, then are ye my disciples indeed" (John 8:31).

We as Christians have taken upon ourselves the name of Jesus. God has given to the Church the authority to use the name of His Son upon the earth.

Jesus said, "And these signs shall follow them that believe; In my name shall they cast out devils; they shall
speak with new tongues; They shall take up serpents;
and if they drink any deadly thing, it shall not hurt
them; they shall lay hands on the sick, and they shall
recover" (Mark 16:17–18).

We are to bear the same fruit that Jesus bore in
His own life (the works I do ye shall do also). Jesus is
saying that God is pleased as we eat at His table and
enter into the joy of His great bountiful supply. The
Lord has made us in His image, but will not be satisfied until we are perfected into His likeness. That means
that we are to enter into His kind of faith the same as
we are to enter into His love. "Beloved, now are we the
sons of God, and . . . when He shall appear, we shall be
like Him; for we shall see Him as He is" (1 John 3:2).
"Because as He is, so are we in this world" (1 John
4:17).

A second witness to this grand truth is the Apostle
Paul. "The spirit itself beareth witness with our spirit,
that we are the children of God: And if children, then
heirs: heirs of God, and joint-heirs with Christ: if so be
that we suffer with Him, that we may be also glorified
together" (Rom. 8:16–17). The one sure reason why
Jesus was God, was because He was the Word of God
incarnate. God has an excellent understanding of why
He makes use of His Word 100 percent of the time.
The reason being, He knows that His Word never fails,
but always accomplishes the thing where unto it is sent
(Isa. 55:11).

That is the exact reason why Jesus has instructed us
to live by, abide in, speak forth and have faith in the
Word of God. No individual can use the Word beyond
the depth where unto he has experienced it, unless for
some specific occasion God gives him a special gift.
But, people will get into trouble if they carelessly ignore their growth in the Word and start banking on
the gift.

The Word is quick and powerful, sharper than any two-edged sword. When the reality of the Word's power and availability awakens within us, then it will manifest outwardly in signs, wonders, miracles, and healing. When we take the time to honor God by saturating our mind, spirit, and tongue with His Word, He will confirm that word which we speak with signs following. "And they went forth, and preached everywhere, the Lord working with them, and confirming the word with signs following" (Mark 16:20).

The psalmist wrote: "Whoso offereth praise glorifieth me: and to him that ordereth his conversation aright will I shew the salvation of God" (Ps. 50:23). Our conversation can take us into the very heart of God; Enoch so ordered his conversation. The Bible tells us that he had the testimony that he pleased God and was translated. What pleased God was Enoch's faith. The Bible is completely clear that faith is birthed out of the Word of God.

Jesus warned us that the way which leadeth to life was narrow. He testified that He is the way, the truth and the life. Therefore, for us to enter fully into the life of God, we must come by the way of the Word. There is the Word we read, the Word we meditate, the Word we sing and praise, the Word we love and share in fellowship, the Word we preach and teach, the Word we pray, and the Word we speak unceasingly. Then there is the rhema of the Word, communicated unto us by the Spirit. When we are filled with the Word, we do not hesitate to release its power which is resident within. Just as Peter when he said, "Silver and gold have I none; but such as I have give I thee: in the name of Jesus Christ of Nazareth rise up and walk" (Acts 3:6). Peter had the gospel Word in him. We read in 1 Thessalonians 1:5, "For our gospel came not in Word only, but also in power, and in the Holy Ghost and in much assurance." The Christian is to be full of both the Spirit and the Word. If we are void of the Spirit we have neither means, nor power where by the Word can be conveyed. The greater the anointing of the Spirit upon us, the more powerful will be the words which we speak. That is why the Scriptures admonish us to walk in the Spirit. For it is there that we will unhesitatingly and boldly speak to our mountains and command them to disappear or to come forth, depending upon the need. When we get careless with our words, then our faith will become weak and unprofitable.

It is interesting to learn just how anointed and powerful the Word of God was in the Book of the Law. "This book of the law shall not depart out of thy mouth; but thou shalt meditate therein day and night, that thou mayest observe to do according to all that is written therein: for then thou shalt make thy way prosperous, and then thou shalt have good success" (Josh. 1:8).

The reason the Christian church is so powerless today is because most Christians are meditating day and night upon everything but the Word of God. How can God be the Christian's Jehova Rapha (the Lord God their healer and physician), unless we are taught the truth that God is the healer and that His heart yearns to stretch forth His hand and touch us? Jesus could not have shown us any plainer than when He healed every one who came to Him.

I have personally witnessed God heal scores and scores of people when I have had the opportunity to pray for them. Sometimes the healing is immediate, sometimes it is gradual. When a fervent prayer, of a man or woman who is willing to pray and speak the word of faith, healing will always be initiated. But, if benefits are to be fully realized the individual prayed for will need to learn to speak the word of healing themselves. Many times the reason for that is, God wants every individual to grow and develop in the law and word of faith.

It is not a question as to whether or not God is willing to do something on someone's behalf. The question is, will the person put themselves in the proper position before God? That position is faith, "For he that cometh to God must believe that He is, and that He is a rewarder of them that diligently seek Him" (Heb. 11:6).

Under the old covenant, the Bible says that during the forty years in the wilderness, there was not one feeble person among them, and the soles of their shoes did not wear out. When the snakes did come, God had Moses lift up a "type of Christ" upon a pole and all who looked upon the brazen serpent were healed.

I have spent some time on healing because I do not wish to see the sick suffer, especially when the true followers of Christ will be banned from society during the time of the "mark of the beast." Jesus is the same yesterday, today and forever (Heb. 13:8). We need only to speak the Word as did He; then our friends, loved ones, and we ourselves will be healed. God desires by the power of His Spirit, as well as by His angels to show Himself strong on our behalf. If we refuse or fail to speak the Word of faith as Jesus said, then we have not because we ask not. Ask He said, that our joy may be full. Faith always settles the matter when the Word is spoken. When we trust God and rejoice in His love and mercy, leaving the results with Him, He said He will bring it to pass.

The result may be instant or it may take a little time. "For ye have need of patience that, after ye have done the will of God, ye might receive the promise; For yet a little while, and He that shall come will come, and will not tarry. Now the just shall live by faith: but if any man draw back, my soul shall have no pleasure in him" (Heb. 10:36–38).

There is no Scripture which more clearly establishes the truth of the word of healing as the following:

> But the path of the just is as the shining light, that shineth more and more unto the perfect day.

> The way of the wicked is as darkness: they know not at what they stumble. [Wickedness is when we do not obey the Word of God.]

> My son, attend to my words; incline thine ear unto my sayings.

> Let them not depart from thine eyes; keep them in the midst of thine heart.

> For they are life unto those that find them, and health to all their flesh.

> Keep thy heart with all diligence; for out of it are the issues of life.

> Put away from thee a froward mouth and perverse lips put far from thee. (Prov. 4:18–24)

In verse 18 it said that the path of the just is as the shining light. Remember, Jesus said that it would be by our own words that we would be justified. The Apostle Paul preached that the just would live by faith. In Jesus we see the Word made flesh. We see the truth of God, and how much He loves His creation. We see in Him what God desires to do for each of us. We learn that God is reachable, touchable, and that He desires to touch us and become involved in every detail of our lives if we will submit to His place of royalty.

Jesus told us, "I am the vine, ye are the branches. He that abideth in me, and I in him, the same bringeth forth much fruit; for without me ye can do nothing" (John 15:5). The Apostle Paul said, "I can do all things through Christ which strengtheneth me" (Phil. 4:13).

One night several years ago when we were living in Independence, Missouri, Jesus spoke to me, "Tell your wife to study my Word." Seven words were all He spoke, but what truth they did contain.

The end of the world is coming. America is staggering like a drunk man on a dark road. We are all in the hands of God's mercy. Just how long He will allow America to remain a sovereign nation we don't completely know. But, the time is running out. We stand on the brink of the world's greatest hour; yet, its saddest. Many will be swept into everlasting salvation in the last grand witness of the gospel. But, on the other hand, untold millions will fall prey to the eternal lie of the devil and perish forever. It hurts to think what is about to happen. We all know that some of those who will fall will be people that we know and love.

Dear Christian who loves the Lord, I can still hear those words which were spoken to me several years ago by the Lord, "Wake up or you will be too late to pray." "Why sleep ye? Rise and pray, lest ye enter into temptation" (Luke 22:46).

Just how much does Jesus really care about you and me. I think the following will tell: when my daughter, Robin, was three years of age she was so in love with Jesus. He seemed to be her whole world at that time in her life. Every night she wanted to hear stories of Jesus. One night when she had said her prayers and I had tucked her into bed, she looked into my face with eyes I had never seen before. She did not move and then she spoke, "Daddy can I see Jesus?" For a moment I paused, her question shook my mind. But, finally I said, "Yes honey you can see Jesus and I will kneel down and ask Him to come and visit you." I never prayed a more sincere prayer than I did that night. When I finished she gave me a kiss and was ready to go to sleep.

When I came home from work three days later she was standing at the screen door waiting for me. As soon as I came into the house she grabbed me by the hand and said, "I want to show you something in my bedroom." She walked over to her bed and patted a certain spot and said, "Daddy, Jesus came to see me last night and this is where He sat. He lifted me up and put me in His lap and talked to me. He let me touch His beard." Does Jesus love this world? Yes, He does, so very, very much.

Maybe He has already come to your house, and your life is filled with His presence. But, if not, He will come if you ask Him. The old hymn many still sing today tells it all so well. "God will take care of you still to the end; Oh what a Father, redeemer, and friend! Jesus will answer whenever you call, He will take care of you, trust Him for all."

Chapter Twelve

"America, America, How Oft Would I Have Gathered You"

We have come to the midnight hour, in the history of man, when gross darkness has covered the earth. But, because there is so much physical light in this modern age, man seems to have lost a great deal of his sensitivity to darkness. There is a song I have always appreciated because it has helped me to retain some of that sensitivity.

> Let us pray for one another for the day is fading fast.
>
> And the night is growing darker, while the scourge goes flaming past.
>
> We can see it in the darkness closing round our narrow way,
>
> And the snares are growing thicker, for each other let us pray.

The sun has been setting upon the "time" of the Gentile nations for almost forty years. The light of the Gentile world has slipped past the horizon and a great darkness of evil is closing upon the world.

We are not spiritually prepared for what is about to befall us. America has led the way into the latter-day Babylon system and has become a nation of sin, where its people have become lovers of pleasure more than lovers of God. The Holy Spirit showed me on two occasions that great tribulation was coming to America.

I recall in one of those experiences just how difficult it was to concentrate on worshipping the Lord, because of the prevailing conditions in the world.

Several years ago when we were living in southern California, a Christian brother and myself would meet each morning at six o'clock to pray. One morning I had awakened; but yielded to the desire for a short nap before leaving, and I went fast to sleep again. Suddenly a loud voice spoke and said, "Wake up you will be too late to pray." Never in my life had anything jolted me with such a shock. Instantly, I was on my feet. I turned to see if my wife was awake, but she was asleep. Needless to say, I left immediately to go and pray. I did not know that our praying each morning meant that much to the Lord. We were seeing a lot of wonderful things happening, both at church and in the lives of our families; but, I did not realize the extent that God was depending upon those prayers to accomplish certain purposes of His will in our lives.

Over the years I have learned that God is absolutely dependent upon our prayers for the accomplishment of His purposes upon the earth. If all the Christians ceased praying, the activity of God would eventually stop in the world.

Today is one clear piece of evidence that this generation of Christians in America have slacked off and have drifted from the deep heartfelt prayer of intercession, to short prayers about this or that. Many do not pray much at all and others none. The spiritual condition in America is reflected in the fact that our hearts do not have a burden for our cities or even our churches. We have tied the hands of God because we have chosen not to pray. I am not speaking of saying a few prayers; rather, the kind of praying where we stay in the presence of God long enough to receive a witness in our spirit.

There is no great mystery in having the anointing of God upon our lives and having the hand of God touch all that we do.

I recall several years ago the faith of a pastor's wife. They were pastoring a small church and many times she would find her cupboards bare. But, she wasn't living by sight, but by faith. When it got on toward mealtime, she would put some water on the stove and get it hot. She testified that not once did the water ever boil out of the pan before God supplied something to put into it. She didn't become distracted by what she did not have. We must safeguard our faith. The Apostle Paul was over into that kind of faith, for he said, "My God shall supply all your needs according to His riches in glory by Christ Jesus" (Phil. 4:19). His faith was abiding in the kingdom which is not of this world. Remember, when we begin to walk with God in the Spirit, He will take us where we are in our faith, and if we let Him, He will develop our faith day by day.

Jesus was not exempt from praying even as we have to do. He would rise a great while before day and spend time with His Father in prayer. If we desire the anointing of love, compassion, and the miracle working power that was in Jesus's life, then we will have to pour out our souls and hearts before God just as He did. Then, live a life that is available to be used by God. We are responsible to provide God with the prayers of faith that He can work with. "Verily, verily, I say unto you, he that believeth on me, the works that I do shall he do also; and greater works than these shall he do; because I go unto my Father" (John 14:12).

A few years ago when I was pastoring a church, a lady dying of cancer came to our meeting. I stood in the prayer meeting that particular morning and spoke to her what I felt the Lord was telling me. I said, "Sister, if you will come back tonight the Lord will heal you," although I would have liked to have seen her

healed right then. But, on the way home the Lord
impressed on me to not eat, but go directly to my
bedroom and stay before Him in prayer that afternoon.

I went in at one o'clock and came out at six o'clock
and we went to church. I called her up, anointed her
with oil, laid hands on her, prayed the prayer of faith
and spoke the word of healing in Jesus' name. Instantly
the cancer died! What do you think would have happened if I had gone home, eaten, taken a nap or turned
the television on: that's right, nothing! The Holy Spirit
will lead us and use us in any situation if we are available. Our availability is greatly dependent upon our
prayer life.

Several years ago our family moved to a town and
I wanted to buy a certain building to hold meetings in.
I was at that time serving the Lord without "purse or
scrip." I remember talking with the real estate man
about the property. He asked me how much money I
had. I said that I didn't have any. He then replied,
"How do you expect to get the building, the seller
wants 25 percent down." I said, "Let's go talk to him."
We walked in and greeted each other. I looked at the
man and spoke these words, "I want to buy your building but I don't have any money." His instant reply was,
"Somehow I knew you didn't, but, I want to sell you
the building. Here is the contract and you can name
your own monthly payments." We signed the contract
and fifteen minutes later the realtor and I left. On the
way back the real estate man turned to me and said,
"The Lord must surely be with you." "Yes," I answered,
"He is."

When we do not know that God is with us and is
willing to work on our behalf, it is simply because we
are not spending enough time with the Lord. All that
America has ever needed is just the Lord, and the
simple willingness to take Him by the hand.

America, in this last generation, has become a nation which has risen up to play. It has set its heart upon fleshly pleasures until there is little feeling after God left within. What happened to Sodom and Gomorrah is happening to America. We have known God as did they, but have not glorified Him as God. We are no longer thankful before Him. We have yielded to the filth of television, videos, sensual music, and idol worship; it has brought upon us a blindness to the lures of the enemy. Without hardly realizing, we have become vain in our imaginations. Gross spiritual darkness has overtaken our hearts.

America is fertile ground for false prophets and every lying strategy of politicians. God has turned America over for great judgment and destruction. Our sins as a nation have reached heaven. The blood of the innocent is crying out against us. It is time, far past the time, for us to repent. Our repentance will not spare the nation, but it will spare many of those we love.

The vain and ungodly have now taken up rule in the land. The restraints of God which once held us together are rapidly disintegrating. Once we held respect for each other and trust in one another. Today, a spirit of rebellion, lawlessness, murder, and fear is spreading like "wild fire" through the land. The whole country is riddled with debt and economic woes of every kind.

Since World War II America has slowly turned her back upon God. What was once sin has now become the norm and now she has lost her way; she is blind, sick, and destitute. Lying upon her deathbed, she is so drunken by the fornication of her deeds that she knows not that her hour of judgment has come. The Church of Laodicea in the Book of Revelation is the Church of the "end." John vividly describes her.

> I know thy works, that thou art neither cold nor
> hot: I would thou wert cold or hot.

So then because thou art lukewarm and neither
cold nor hot, I will spew thee out of my mouth.

Because thou sayest, I am rich, and increased
with goods, and have need of nothing; and
knowest not that thou art wretched, and miser-
able, and poor, and blind, and naked:

I counsel thee to buy of me gold tried in the
fire, that thou mayest be rich; and white rai-
ment, that thou mayest be clothed, and that the
shame of thy nakedness do not appear; and
anoint thine eyes with eye-salve, that thou mayest
see.

As many as I love, I rebuke and chasten: be
zealous therefore, and repent. (Rev. 3:15–19)

This condition of Laodicea so tragically pictures
the churches of America. They have lost their power
with God. The intercessors have vacated the altar. There
are so very few who are daily travailing in prayer for
the power of the Blood of Jesus to come upon their
homes, churches, and communities.

A great sleep has overtaken most of the Christian
churches in America. The altars are all but forsaken.
Our love for God has waxed cold. The love for the
world has overtaken our hearts. We cannot pull ourselves away from the drugging powers of our society.
We have fallen deep into an apostasy of the spirit. Not
many pastors can discern between the saved and the
unsaved. Many are more concerned about their handicap on the golf course than the spiritual handicap of
their flock.

There has been a massive retreat from the holy
standards of the Bible. There are only a few pastors
who care enough to go into the homes of their sheep
and labor for their souls. A great state of compromise
with the spirit of the age has reached astronomical
proportions. A fresh word anointed with God's power

is no longer spiritually correct (such a word is unpopular) the pastor would be placed in a position of judging the spiritual condition of His own flock. Today, in America, very few pastors are spending enough time in prayer to have the strength and concern of heart which can bring God's spiritual judgment and correction to bear in the house of God.

A great apostasy is in the making all across America. The spirit of the world has flooded the homes and minds of Christians. There seems to be little alarm that daily communion is occurring between demons and believers. Rock music (including Christian rock) in all forms can be heard in almost every home. Hours of wasted time is spent in front of the television set where the Christian is being entertained by the spirit of the beast.

The words of the prophet Joel must no longer go unheeded. To you and I are his words spoken: "Sanctify a fast, call a solemn assembly: Gather the people, sanctify the congregation, assemble the elders, gather the children . . . let . . . the ministers of the Lord, weep between the porch and the altar" (Joel 2:15–17).

I can envision Jesus even now on the hill overlooking our nation's capitol weeping and saying to us, "O America, O America why have you rejected me, how oft would I have gathered you, as a hen gathereth her chicks under her wings, but you would not. Behold your land shall become desolate, even a place of sorrow, tears, and death."

Where is the weeping and mourning for America, who is so afflicted, chained, and soon to perish. With her will fall millions of unsuspecting Christians. Only a fiercely united band of praying intercessors can turn the battle to the gate. It is too late for talk, social activities, recreational programs, and bazaars. Unless God breaks up our hearts, makes them as fallow ground, where we can once again weep for the souls of men, we ourselves are in the gravest danger of being swept into the deceiving darkness that now covers the earth.

Christians, we are in our Gethsemane—the hour of judgment has come—and that judgment has begun at the house of God. Our only hope is from above. Follow carefully the account of Jesus in Gethsemane.

> And when He was at the place, He said unto them, pray that ye enter not into temptation.
>
> And He was withdrawn from them about a stone's cast, and kneeled down, and prayed,
>
> Saying, Father, if thou be willing, remove this cup from me: nevertheless not my will, but thine, be done.
>
> And there appeared an angel unto Him from heaven, strengthening Him.
>
> And being in an agony He prayed more earnestly: and His sweat was as it were great drops of blood falling down to the ground.
>
> And when He rose up from prayer, and was come to His disciples, He found them sleeping for sorrow.
>
> And said unto them, why sleep ye? Rise and pray, lest ye enter into temptation.
>
> And while He yet spake, behold a multitude, and he that was called Judas, one of the twelve, went before them, and drew near unto Jesus to kiss Him. (Luke 22:40–47)

The foregoing Scriptures tells us as Jesus prayed, an angel from heaven came and strengthened Him. I do not need to tell you that if Jesus needed an angel to strengthen Him how great then is our need and how great will that need increase during the days that lie ahead. A prayer life, liken unto the prayer life of Jesus, will bring down angels to our side.

Jesus said, "Why sleep ye? Rise and pray, lest ye enter into temptation" (Luke 22:47). All the disciples of Jesus failed under the great temptation. They all lost their testimony and gave up on their calling. Peter was tempted to lie and he did. They barely escaped that hour which came upon them, so great was the temptation to think first of themselves. They were walking close to Jesus when it struck, but were not "crucified with Christ" (Gal. 2:20).

What we are about to face will be seven times hotter. We have been warned by the Word of God. Great trials and testings are coming upon the people of God. But, God has promised that those who would keep the word of His patience, He would keep them from the hour of temptation, which has now come upon the world to try those that dwell upon the earth (Rev. 3:10).

Jesus has warned us just how spiritually devastating this great trial will be. It can cost us our names in the Book of Life. We must overcome the spirits of pleasure, coldness, fear, lust, greed, compromise, and false doctrines which are even now at our doors and already resident in the hearts of many Christians. How important it is at this present moment to pray for one another, for the day is fading fast. We must quickly disassociate ourselves from the world, it reeks with death. Spiritual death controls the world and all its desires. We must separate ourselves from all that is in and of the world until we have no longing for it. God warns us, "Love not the world, neither the things that are in the world" (1 John 2:15).

Unless we sever our emotional ties to the world and replace them with a pure affection on the things of God, dear Christian, we will be overcome by this temptation that is coming. You and I will not be able to lay down our lives for Jesus (Rev. 6). We will not be able to avoid the world's system and its economic pres-

sure. Jesus said, "Remember Lot's wife. Whosoever
shall seek to save his life shall lose it" (Luke 17:32–33).
"Even thus shall it be in the day when the son of man
is revealed" (Luke 17:30).

We are going to be as tempted as was Lot's wife to
take one last compromising look in the face of the
most deceptive tribulation this world will ever witness.
What we will see, will create consternation in our hearts.
Jesus said that men's hearts would fail them. The heart
of a Christian should be his great bastion of faith, his
reservoir of strength and the place where Jesus reigns.
The church in America is about to face her Gethsemane
without the slightest thought of her crucifixion which
lies ahead.

What little faith we might have will quickly dissi-
pate when the second beast begins to spew fire out of
his mouth. We are at this present time entering the eve
of this dark hour. Already there has risen in the land
men with deep cunning, wolves in sheep's clothing,
men like animals without a conscience waiting to de-
vour the innocent and the weak.

Jesus warned His elect that when this great tribulation broke upon the world, that there had never been
anything like it, not since the beginning of the world,
nor ever would there be again (Matt. 24:21).

Many Christians are in debt, and deeply dependent
upon the world's system. Millions are materially locked
into the present economic snare and have no plans to
free themselves from its grasp. If we are living by sight
now and we are not preparing ourselves to soon live by
faith, what shall become of us in the midst of a sudden
transition.

It is time to pray and cry out to God for Him to
brood over us, making us ready for the great struggle
our souls must endure. He alone can prepare us. We
must know that God is first with us and that He dwells
within us. We must know His voice so we can be led

by His spirit. We must have the knowledge of His power and boldly be able to speak the word of faith. We must be able to pray the prayer of faith in any situation. But, most of all, we must be able to abide in the spirit of God's love. How great will be the temptation to revile, fight, and even kill for the things we have worked all our lives for. Remember, Jesus said that He did not have a place to lay His head.

When the ax of the beast falls upon the world, for the Christian, there will be no supermarkets, no hospitals, no bank accounts, little or no transportation. We may lose everything we ever held dear or took for granted in this world. Great trouble is coming. The devil has come down in great wrath upon the world, knowing he has only a few days left (Rev. 12).

The spirit of the anti-Christ can be seen and felt presently in every town and hamlet. Great evil is going before the beast as a wind before the rain. This evil is overtaking our country, our churches, our schools, and our lives. The men and women of God have grown weak in a time in which they should be strong. They have forgotten that the Lord is their strength, and that the anointing of that strength comes as we spend precious time in His presence.

Dear saint of God, it is time to pray and pour out our souls to God, until we can feel His strong arms about us, and know with an assurance that we are walking in His will. Yes, we only have a very short moment to "flee to that 'Rock' which is higher than I," and find shelter in the covenant of His Blood. Then we will be able to say with David of old,

> Yea, though I walk through the valley of the shadow of death, I will fear no evil: for thou art with me; thy rod (the Word) and thy staff (the Holy Spirit) they comfort me. Thou preparest a table before me in the presence of mine enemies: thou anointest my head with oil; my cup

runneth over. Surely goodness and mercy shall
follow me all the days of my life: and I will dwell
in the house of the Lord for ever. (Ps. 23:4–6)

We are not ready for what is imminently coming
upon the earth unless we can say with the Apostle Paul,
"For to me to live is Christ, and to die is gain" (Phil.
1:21). I am not sure that we all know our hearts, and
whether or not we are ready to lay down our lives for
Jesus as He laid down His life for us. Shadrach, Meshach,
and Abednigo were under the old covenant, yet they
wavered not in the face of death. They told the king to
his face that they would not serve other gods, nor
worship his "image." King Nebuchadnezzar watched as
the furnace was heated seven times hotter. These
Hebrew sons would not have ever known the deliver-
ing hand of their God had their hearts failed them
because of fear.

If they had put themselves above the covenant they
had with God and compromised just a little, they may
have escaped the fiery furnace of Nebuchadnezzar, but
they would not have escaped the fiery furnace of hell.
To turn away from God in the presence of the enemy
is the highest treason that one can commit. Such an
outright rejection of God will automatically sever our
covenant with Him. The temptation to do this is going
to be overpowering to those who are not walking in
full surrender to the Lord Jesus Christ.

This end-time Babylonian beast has already made
deep inroads into the body of Christ. He is preparing
the Christian for the slaughter. Jesus said that we must
watch therefore and pray always that we may possess
the strength to escape these things. This spirit of the
beast is attacking us where we live. He is cumbering us
with loads of cares. The average Christian is burdened
down, needing money for this and money for that
(college education, insurance, house payments, taxes,
food, transportation, and debts, to name a few). Many

have just enough faith to get them from one payday to
the next before panic sets in. It is not God's will that
His people allow themselves to foolishly submit to the
bondage of debt. But we reason, that is the only way
I can get what I want. Is it?

The devil has cunningly taken America into every
conceivable bondage possible. He has carefully deceived
the Christians into developing a great dependency upon
the government and its welfare programs. We have
been brainwashed to believe that more government
regulations and visa cards are a necessity in today's
world. Every day the net is getting tighter and tighter,
until, when Satan strikes the final blow, Christians will
be caught in this web of dependence upon charge and
pay while the government regulates the way. Satan knew
such a deceptive lifestyle would leave a person weak
and destitute of faith.

But, the deception did not stop there. Satan saw to
it that a lying doctrine would be spread throughout the
world, that before any such hell would ever manifest
upon the earth, all the Christians would be raptured
away to heaven. Jesus taught no such doctrine. What
He did teach was not to let that day come upon us
unaware.

Those who are not discerning the signs of the times
will feel that the only sensible thing to do is to trust the
government and society so they can have the benefits
of a doctor, food, and employment for their families.
Once the economic trap is set and the Christians have
embraced the hand of Babylon's blessing, then there
will be issued a seemingly harmless little card or a
number to be used at the grocery stores and elsewhere. The dependency upon the government will be
so complete that many will see the snare as just another governmental program, instead of the long foretold deception which Satan would bring upon the world.

God said He would make us a way of escape. Moses would have never gotten the Israelites out of Egypt had it not been for the oppression of Pharaoh. But, because their trials were so bitter and the suffering so sore, they were willing to listen to what their God-sent deliverer had to say. But, before they could cross the sea they had to be separated from Egypt. God had to perform a great and mighty work before they were freed. The Hebrews had to face death itself before the final victory came. There was only one way they could overcome, and that was by the blood. The plan of God has not changed today. Those who escape the Egypt of this hour will do so through the Blood of the Lamb, as the Flesh of the Lamb (the Word) is fully digested within.

The Israelites could not have imagined that God would do or could do such a thing when He opened a path in the sea. The personal leader that day was Moses. Today, our leader is Jesus through the Holy Spirit. The Israelites who made it into the protection of the sea, were those who heard and obeyed the voice of Moses. Today those who will make it into the sea of God's end-time saving grace and experience God's supernatural power on their behalf, will be those who will hear the voice of the Spirit and follow Him wherever He shall lead. God has a way prepared for us. The display of His power will be far greater, and the victory more glorious. But, the battle is yet to be won.

The prophet Daniel declared that God will be our God in such a time as we face. But, God cannot be our God if we continue to idle our time away and allow the precious moments in which we should be preparing slip away. Redeem the time as never before. We must prove ourselves as worthy ministers in the execution of His Word. We must bear a faithful witness and never let pass an opportunity to tell the perishing world of the impending disaster and the way of escape.

What would Jesus do and how much different would be His lifestyle if He were physically here today. His spiritual life would be altered none, His prayers would continue. The daily pouring out of His life in ministry would remain the same. He would continue to heal the sick, cast out demons, and teach the uncompromised Word. He most certainly would be warning the world of its coming judgment as He did to His people, for He knows millions will perish if they reject Him. He would be weeping over America, trying to gather her into the arms of His love.

We must be prepared with the whole armor of God to fight the greatest spiritual battle of our lives. We may not feel like praying; pray anyway. Ask God for His help, for His guidance, for His strength; for Him to bless you, your children, your neighbors, your pastor. The spirit to pray will grow within you until your heart will be drawn out to prayer. The fire of God's love will fill your heart as you stay faithful in prayer. Remember, Jesus is interceding on our behalf. I have to believe that all of heaven will be on their knees with us in mighty prayer until the victory is won and the final conflict is over.

The Apostle John would want us to find strength in the words the Spirit gave him to give to us, many centuries ago.

> But that which ye have already hold fast till I come. And he that overcometh, and keepeth my works unto the end, to him will I give power over the nations: and he shall rule them with a rod of iron; as the vessels of a potter shall they be broken to shivers: even as I received of my Father. And I will give him the morning star. (Rev. 2:25–28)

Jesus said to His disciples, "Tarry ye in Jerusalem until ye be endued with power from on high." Today can be no different, we all must have the Baptism of the Holy Ghost and be filled with the power of God. Jesus told His disciples that after the Holy Ghost came upon them, they would be witnesses of Him. It is in and through the baptism of the Spirit that communion between us and God is opened wide.

God's people are going to need all the gifts of the Holy Spirit in this last hour we are passing through. We received Jesus by faith for our salvation. It is by the same faith, as our heart hungers before God, that He will fill us to overflowing with the abundance of His love, joy, wisdom, grace, and power for the express purpose that we may run the race that is now set before us. That, we may be a valiant soldier in this final conflict of the church age.

We must be filled with the spirit of God's anointing power to overcome. Jesus told us that some of the virgins would be foolish, and for one reason or another would not see to it that they had oil sufficient in their lamps. May you and I have a heart as did David of old which did pant after God as the deer after the water brook.

I began this chapter with the first stanza of a song which seems to speak so well to our times. I would like to close with the last three stanzas.

> We are walking down time's vista; we are very near the end;
> Let us pray that God, the Father, may His guiding Spirit send.
> Now the foe becomes more daring, knowing well the latter day,
> Tis the strength of His despairing; for each other let us pray.
>
> Pray in faith, and pray unceasing, to the God we love and trust,
> For our prayers are much availing if we walk upright and just.

Be not weary of exhorting, heed the lesson of
each day
And that we may be unwavering, for each other
let us pray.

It is waning on toward midnight, soon we'll
hear the watchman say,
See? The son of God is coming; go and meet
Him on the way.
That our lamps may then be burning bright
enough to guide the way,
And that we may share His glory, for each other
let us pray.

                                        —David Smith

The Burning
of a
Strange Fire

by Barney Fuller

This fascinating book takes the reader into the true origins of Mormonism.

Mr. Fuller is a descendant of several generations of Mormons. He spent many years as a Mormon Elder. His ground-breaking book will help readers understand the mysteries that gave birth to this religion.

To Order Write: (Price: $10.00)

Daniel's House
Box 329
Riverside, TX 77367

We welcome comments from our readers. Feel free to write to us at the following address:

Editorial Department
Huntington House Publishers
P.O. Box 53788
Lafayette, LA 70505

More Good Books from Huntington House

The Best of HUMAN EVENTS
Fifty Years of Conservative
Thought and Action
Edited by James C. Roberts

Before Ronald Reagan, before Barry Goldwater, since the closing days of World War II, HUMAN EVENTS stood against the prevailing winds of the liberal political Zeitgeist. HUMAN EVENTS has published the best of three generations of conservative writers—academics, journalists, philosophers, politicians: Frank Chodorov and Richard Weaver, Henry Hazlitt and Hans Sennholz, William F. Buckley and M. Stanton Evans, Jack Kemp and Dan Quayle. A representative sample of their work, marking fifty years of American political and social history, is here collected in a single volume.

ISBN 1-56384-018-9 $34.95 Hardback

Can Families Survive in Pagan America?
by Samuel Dresner

Drug addiction, child abuse, divorce, and the welfare state have dealt terrible, pounding blows to the family structure. At the same time, robbery, homicide, and violent assaults have increased at terrifying rates. But, according to the author, we can restore order to our country and our lives. Using the tenets of Jewish family life and faith, Dr. Dresner calls on Americans from every religion and walk of life to band together and make strong, traditional families a personal and national priority again—before it's too late.

ISBN Trade Paper: 1-56384-080-4 $15.99
Hardcover: 1-56384-086-3 $31.99

Out of Control— Who's Watching Our Child Protection Agencies?
by Brenda Scott

This book of horror stories is true. The deplorable and unauthorized might of Child Protection Services is capable of reaching into and destroying any home in America. No matter how innocent and happy your family may be, you are one accusation away from disaster. Social workers are allowed to violate constitutional rights and often become judge, jury, and executioner. Innocent parents may appear on computer registers and be branded "child abuser" for life. Every year, it is estimated that over 1 million people are falsely accused of child abuse in this country. You could be next, says author and speaker Brenda Scott.

ISBN 1-56384-069-3 $9.99

Beyond Political Correctness: Are There Limits to This Lunacy?
by David Thibodaux

Author of the best-selling *Political Correctness: The Cloning of the American Mind,* Dr. David Thibodaux now presents his long awaited sequel—*Beyond Political Correctness: Are There Limits to This Lunacy?* The politically correct movement has now moved beyond college campuses. The movement has succeeded in turning the educational system of this country into a system of indoctrination. Its effect on education was predictable: steadily declining scores on every conceivable test which measures student performance; and, increasing numbers of college freshmen who know a great deal about condoms, homosexuality, and abortion, but whose basic skills in language, math, and science are alarmingly deficient.

ISBN 1-56384-066-9 $9.99

Political Correctness: The Cloning of the American Mind
by David Thibodaux, Ph.D.

The author, a professor of literature at the University of Southwestern Louisiana, confronts head on the movement that is now being called Political Correctness. Political correctness, says Thibodaux, "is an umbrella under which advocates of civil rights, gay and lesbian rights, feminism, and environmental causes have gathered." To incur the wrath of these groups, one only has to disagree with them on political, moral, or social issues. To express traditionally Western concepts in universities today can result in not only ostracism, but even suspension. (According to a recent "McNeil-Lehrer News Hour" report, one student was suspended for discussing the reality of the moral law with an avowed homosexual. He was reinstated only after he apologized.)

ISBN 1-56384-026-X Trade Paper $9.99

ORDER THESE HUNTINGTON HOUSE BOOKS !

- America Betrayed—Marlin Maddoux....................................7.99
- The Assault—Dale A. Berryhill...9.99
- Beyond Political Correctness—David Thibodaux.........................9.99
- The Best of HUMAN EVENTS—Edited by James C. Roberts..............34.95
- Bleeding Hearts and Propaganda—James R. Spencer....................9.99
- Can Families Survive in Pagan America?—Samuel Dresner..............15.99
- Circle of Death—Richmond Odom.....................................10.99
- Combat Ready—Lynn Stanley...9.99
- Conservative, American & Jewish—Jacob Neusner.......................9.99
- The Dark Side of Freemasonry—Ed Decker..............................9.99
- The Demonic Roots of Globalism—Gary Kah...........................10.99
- Don't Touch That Dial—Barbara Hattemer & Robert Showers.....9.99/19.99 HB
- En Route to Global Occupation—Gary Kah.............................9.99
- Everyday Evangelism—Ray Comfort...................................10.99
- *Exposing the AIDS Scandal—Dr. Paul Cameron....................7.99/2.99
- Freud's War with God—Jack Wright, Jr.................................7.99
- Gays & Guns—John Eidsmoe...................................7.99/14.99 HB
- Global Bondage—Cliff Kincaid......................................10.99
- Goddess Earth—Samantha Smith..9.99
- Health Begins in Him—Terry Dorian...................................9.99
- Heresy Hunters—Jim Spencer..8.99
- Hidden Dangers of the Rainbow—Constance Cumbey.....................9.99
- High-Voltage Christianity—Michael Brown............................10.99
- High on Adventure—Stephen Arrington.................................8.99
- Homeless in America—Jeremy Reynalds.................................9.99
- How to Homeschool (Yes, You!)—Julia Toto............................3.99
- Hungry for God—Larry E. Myers.......................................9.99
- I Shot an Elephant in My Pajamas—Morrie Ryskind w/ John Roberts......12.99
- *Inside the New Age Nightmare—Randall Baer.....................9.99/2.99
- A Jewish Conservative Looks at Pagan America—Don Feder.....9.99/19.99 HB
- Journey into Darkness—Stephen Arrington.............................9.99
- Kinsey, Sex and Fraud—Dr. Judith A. Reisman & Edward Eichel........11.99
- The Liberal Contradiction—Dale A. Berryhill.........................9.99
- Legalized Gambling—John Eidsmoe.....................................7.99
- Loyal Opposition—John Eidsmoe.......................................8.99
- The Media Hates Conservatives—Dale A. Berryhill...........9.99/19.99 HB
- New Gods for a New Age—Richmond Odom................................9.99
- One Man, One Woman, One Lifetime—Rabbi Reuven Bulka.................7.99
- Out of Control—Brenda Scott................................9.99/19.99 HB
- Outcome-Based Education—Peg Luksik & Pamela Hoffecker..............9.99
- The Parched Soul of America—Leslie Kay Hedger w/ Dave Reagan......10.99
- Please Tell Me—Tom McKenney...9.99
- Political Correctness—David Thibodaux...............................9.99
- Resurrecting the Third Reich—Richard Terrell........................9.99
- Revival: Its Principles and Personalities—Winkie Pratney...........10.99

*Available in Salt Series

Available at bookstores everywhere or order direct from:
Huntington House Publishers • P.O. Box 53788 • Lafayette, LA 70505
Send check/money order. For faster service use VISA/MASTERCARD.
Call toll-free 1-800-749-4009.
Add: Freight and handling, $3.50 for the first book ordered, and $.50 for
each additional book up to 5 books.